RICHARD HOOKER

CASCADE COMPANIONS

The Christian theological tradition provides an embarrassment of riches: from scripture to modern scholarship, we are blessed with a vast and complex theological inheritance. And yet this feast of traditional riches is too frequently inaccessible to the general reader.

The Cascade Companions series addresses the challenge by publishing books that combine academic rigor with broad appeal and readability. They aim to introduce nonspecialist readers to that vital storehouse of authors, documents, themes, histories, arguments, and movements that comprise this heritage with brief yet compelling volumes.

TITLES IN THIS SERIES:

Reading Paul by Michael J. Gorman
Theology and Culture by D. Stephen Long
Creation and Evolution by Tatha Wiley
Theological Interpretation of Scripture by Stephen Fowl
Reading Bonhoeffer by Geffrey B. Kelly
Justpeace Ethics by Jarem Sawatsky
Feminism and Christianity by Caryn D. Griswold
Angels, Worms, and Bogeys by Michelle A. Clifton-Soderstrom
Christianity and Politics by C. C. Pecknold
A Way to Scholasticism by Peter S. Dillard
Theological Theodicy by Daniel Castelo
The Letter to the Hebrews in Social-Scientific Perspective by David A. deSilva
Basil of Caesarea by Andrew Radde-Galwitz
A Guide to St. Symeon the New Theologian by Hannah Hunt
Reading John by Christopher W. Skinner
Forgiveness by Anthony Bash
Jeremiah by Jack Lundbom
John Calvin by Donald K. McKim

RICHARD HOOKER

A Companion to His Life and Work

W. BRADFORD LITTLEJOHN

CASCADE *Books* · Eugene, Oregon

RICHARD HOOKER
A Companion to His Life and Work

Copyright © 2015 W. Bradford Littljohn. All rights reserved. Except for brief quotations in critical publications or reviews, no part of this book may be reproduced in any manner without prior written permission from the publisher. Write: Permissions, Wipf & Stock, 199 W. 8th Ave., Eugene, OR 97401.

Cascade Books
An Imprint of Wipf and Stock Publishers
199 W. 8th Ave., Suite 3
Eugene, OR 97401
www.wipfandstock.com

ISBN 13: 978-1-62564-735-1

Cataloging-in-Publication data:

Littlejohn, W. Bradford.

Richard Hooker : a companion to his life and work.

xvi + 206 p. ; cm. Includes bibliographical references.

ISBN 13: 978-1-62564-735-1

1. Theology, 2. Richard Hooker, 3. Anglican Theology. I. Title.

BT2665.3 E49 2012

Manufactured in the U.S.A.

CONTENTS

Acknowledgments • vii

Preface • xiii

1 **Richard Hooker: The Myth** • 1
2 **Richard Hooker: The Man** • 15
3 **Richard Hooker: The Book** • 32
4 **Hooker as Protestant** • 52
5 **Hooker as Polemicist** • 69
6 **Hooker as Philosopher** • 81
7 **Hooker as Pastor** • 93
8 **Key Themes: Scripture** • 110
9 **Key Themes: Law** • 128
10 **Key Themes: Church** • 147
11 **Key Themes: Liturgy and Sacraments** • 163
12 **Richard Hooker: Contemporary** • 184

Bibliography • 197

PREFACE

IN AN AGE WHEN nearly two million new books are being published each year, it's not easy for us authors to justify the addition of one more to the heap, however much it may flatter our vanity. And with so many books and articles on Hooker already out there (see the bibliography for a small selection), why another one? What do I hope to achieve with this book? Well, three things, I suppose.

First, I hope to introduce Hooker to audiences that have barely heard of him, if at all. It is a sad fact that a great many educated, intelligent, theologically-interested readers, especially in North America, fall into this category. Although Hooker is being written about today more than ever, with the segmentation of disciplines and the growing divide between church and academy, he is being read about by fewer and fewer non-specialists. Perhaps the tide has begun to turn on that front; I am not sure. In any case, I hope this book will contribute to that turning of the tide. Even if I had little new to say about Hooker, if publishing a new book meant that more people got to know him (since people always buy new books sooner than old books), it might not be wasted effort.

Of course, while I would like all people everywhere to get to know Hooker, I have my own context, North American evangelicalism and Reformed churches, particularly in mind. Most of what has been written and read about Hooker, it seems, has remained confined to the Anglican

Preface

Communion, which claims him for its own, and not unreasonably so. But it is unfortunate that so many Protestants in other traditions should have so thoroughly conceded him to the Anglicans as not to even bother reading him. Few theologians, I wager, have so much to teach American evangelicals.

Not that I have written either explicitly from or to that context. I hope that readers of all backgrounds, not least Anglicans of various stripes, will find this survey accessible, timely, and relevant (although perhaps occasionally iconoclastic). The focus is broad, and I try not to presume too much prior knowledge on the part of readers. The Reformation, and the English Reformation in particular, is rarely and barely understood nowadays, and I have made some effort to contextualize Hooker's life and thought against this crucial backdrop—the tumultuous seven decades before he began to write—rather than simply plunging into his ideas on their own. There is of course so much more that clamors to be said in each chapter to provide the full context, and no room to say it, but I hope the footnotes, directing readers to valuable further reading where helpful, will be sufficient.

Second, I hope to digest for general audiences—including general academic audiences—some of the fruits of the extraordinary recent renaissance of Hooker scholarship, which has till now been mostly confined to specialist academic publications and journals. To be sure, one other recent book has tried to do that, Charles Miller's *Richard Hooker and the Vision of God: Exploring the Origins of "Anglicanism."* Readers comparing this book with that one, however, will note several important differences, both of objective and interpretation. Miller's target audience, in any case, is a somewhat narrower one: the Church of England seminarian, above all. And he aspires to derive a much more complete "systematic theology" from Hooker than I do here. In any case, though, the task of distilling the torrents of recent scholarship is a formidable one. Few readers can be expected to have patience for the tedious and sometimes seemingly abstruse debates that Hooker scholars of necessity must concern themselves with, and yet the outcome of these debates does make quite a difference for what sort of thinker we take Hooker to be; one simply cannot try to present a "least common denominator" Hooker, a portrait of Hooker that all would agree on. For, beyond the basic biographical details, there is little, it seems, that everyone agrees on.

I am thus left with the choice of either engaging in detail with the secondary literature in these pages, and thus losing the interest of the readers (not to mention running out of space very quickly), or simply presenting my own reading, without meeting objections or refuting rival readings in any detail. I have opted for an untidy mixture of these two approaches, or, to put it more positively, a *via media*. I have tried, especially in chapters 1, 4 and 5, to orient the reader to the major debates and key names in recent Hooker scholarship, and to make clear what is at stake in these debates—how they really do shape what sort of Hooker we are dealing with, and what, if anything, he has to offer today's church. I have not hesitated to criticize those that, in my judgment, are methodologically flawed, insufficiently attentive to Hooker's context, or simply bad readers of the text. Indeed, in treating several key points of Hooker's theology, especially in part 3 of this book, I have to engage these flawed readings directly, in order to situate and clarify my own reading of Hooker and why it matters. The result may be at times a bit too much detail for general readers, and will certainly be too little detail for other Hooker scholars, who might be itching to challenge my interpretations at certain points. On most of these points,

Preface

I hope some of my other published work will help in filling out arguments I can only sketch here. In any case, I have tried to avoid cramming more detail into the footnotes, which would merely add distraction for little gain.

I have also tried to avoid false objectivity. It will not take long for readers to realize that I am a great admirer of Hooker, that I find both his style and the content of his arguments profoundly satisfying more often than not, and that I hope to heartily commend him to Christians today as a valuable role model and teacher. I do not seek to whitewash his imperfections, or skew his views to align with my own, so this is certainly no hagiography. I seek to say nothing about Hooker that is not, from all I have been able to determine, amply supported by a close reading of his work and of his historical context. But neither do I pretend to be a mere historian (if there is such a thing), describing Hooker with the detached objectivity of a biologist dissecting a fruit fly.

This admission, and the swipes that I take at some prevalent readings of Hooker in the course of this book, will invite the charge, I am sure, that I am simply trying to recast Hooker in my own preferred mold. I read Hooker as a more or less irenic Reformed theologian, some will say, because that's what I myself hope to be, and I would love to have Hooker on my side. I cannot wholly put to rest such objections in advance, I am sure; the proof must be in the pudding, that is, in the persuasiveness of my reading of the texts. But if it helps, the fact is that when I first read Hooker, I didn't want him to be particularly Reformed, nor was I friendly to many of the views that I attribute to him in this book. My own theological and indeed historical understanding changed dramatically in the course of reading and studying Hooker, and I hope yours will as well; he has much to offer almost any thoughtful reader.

Preface

This leads to my last point. This book is meant to be a *companion* to Richard Hooker, not a substitute. Having finished this brief introduction, the best thing you can do is to read Hooker himself, savoring him slowly in small but frequent portions. His distinctive style is difficult to penetrate at first but can be downright enchanting once you grow familiar with it. Critical editions of his writings are fantastically expensive, but some decent inexpensive facsimile reprints are available, and the whole text of the *Laws* is available online at the Online Library of Liberty.[1]

Since I am not seeking to tell you all about Hooker, then, but simply help you get to know him for yourself, this has freed me up to take a sort of snapshot approach in this slim volume. I make no pretensions to systematic completeness; in particular, the four "key themes" chapters, while obviously singling out themes central to Hooker's theology and still relevant to us today, clearly leave out other very important topics. Space permitting, I should have said a great deal about Hooker's soteriology—his account of justification and sanctification, and of course predestination. He certainly has some new and interesting things to say on these subjects, though not perhaps as novel as many interpreters have suggested. But these are particularly complex topics, not perhaps well suited for the quick flyover approach of this book, and you will have to make do with footnotes pointing you toward further reading on these issues.

Finally, a brief note about notes, and about spelling. To avoid crowding the text with footnotes, I have simply used parenthetical notes for all references to Hooker's magnum opus, *The Laws of Ecclesiastical Polity*, which I quote

1. See http://oll.libertyfund.org/people/richard-hooker.

Preface

from and cite far more than any other source. I have used the traditional format of Book # (or "Pref." for the Preface), chapter number, section number (so, I.2.3, VIII.5.1, etc.), which will generally get you to the right spot in any edition, including the online edition (with a few exceptions, which I note when relevant). For Hooker's other writings, which appear in vols. 4 and 5 of the Folger Library Edition of Hooker's works, I have used that edition for citations, with the abbreviation *FLE*, followed by volume number and page number. When quoting Hooker, I have taken the liberty of modernizing all spelling and in some cases punctuation and capitalization. There is no reason that it should be easier for modern readers to read Calvin, a sixteenth-century Frenchman, than Hooker, a sixteenth-century Englishman, just because the first has been translated into modern English, and the second left in archaic English. Hooker's style is a formidable challenge enough for the modern reader; no need to complicate the task with odd spelling.

With these housekeeping matters out of the way, let's get to Richard Hooker himself. I hope you find him as engaging a companion as I have these past five years.

Brad Littlejohn
Good Friday, 2015
Bucer's Coffeehouse
Moscow, ID

ACKNOWLEDGMENTS

As the Beatles said, "I get by with a little help from my friends," and it is as true when it comes to scholarship as it is anywhere—or perhaps more true, as much as we academics try to hide it sometimes. I owe much of what little I know to the conversations and lessons of friends and mentors, not to the books I've read—which I often only read because a friend or mentor told me to. So it was with Hooker himself, and so it has been with most of the books and articles that have enriched my knowledge of Hooker, the Puritans, and the Reformation. Those who have helped me along the way are too numerous to thank here, but my doctoral advisors, Oliver and Joan O'Donovan, assuredly deserve more credit than anyone. They encouraged me to develop an affection for Hooker but never let me take that affection for granted, insisting that I thoroughly defend my readings and interpretations at every point. They also never let me take my love of writing for granted, forcing me over and over to "omit needless words," as Strunk and White have been exhorting me for many years.

Torrance Kirby has been an attentive and constructive critic, reader, and friend throughout my last few years of study, and I am but one of a whole generation of young scholars indebted to his boundless energy, remarkable scholarship, and iconoclastic opinions. Paul Avis read and commented on both my dissertation and the draft of this book, and although he certainly wouldn't agree with

Acknowledgments

everything I write, has been encouraging and constructive at every point. His watchful eye has saved me from many infelicitous expressions.

My friendship with Peter Escalante began at the exact same time as my acquaintance with Hooker, and both have grown together, and enriched one another, over the past five years; his erudition has almost without fail directed me to just the source I needed to acquaint myself with a new area of study, or tackle some interpretive difficulty. It has also been a delight to explore Hooker together with Andrew Fulford over the past few years, and I look forward to the many publications with which he will no doubt soon be enriching the field of Hooker studies. His careful reading of the draft of this book was a great help. Dan Graves and Joseph Minich also read and commented on the complete text, offering many words of encouragement and suggestions for improvement.

I am grateful also to all the members of the Richard Hooker Society, and to the many stimulating conference conversations and email exchanges with them that have broadened and deepened my grasp of Hooker, and just as importantly, of the current state of scholarly conversation. I am also happy to be able to call my friends such remarkable emerging Reformation scholars as Eric Parker, Michael Lynch, Eric Hutchinson, Davey Henreckson, and Jordan Ballor, who have done much to stimulate and clarify some of the insights that have gone into this book. And perhaps the most direct thanks is due to my friend Christian Amondson, the editor at Cascade who asked me to write a totally different book and then cheerily agreed the moment I suggested writing this one instead. He has been wonderful to work with (and extraordinarily forgiving of delays) on many projects over the past seven years, and I look forward to many more.

Acknowledgments

Most of all, of course, I thank my wife Rachel, for her extraordinary longsuffering in the face of my stubborn dedication to such impecunious tasks as writing a book for American evangelicals about a long-dead English theologian. Besides being a support and encouragement throughout all of my scholarly endeavors, she was a particular help with this one, patiently listening to my first drafts in the evening and staunchly insisting that I do something about that overly-florid prose that I kept indulging in. For that, I'm sure many readers will be grateful as well. My three children, Soren, Pippa, and Oliver, have been a delight to me every evening at the end of work, reminding me that for all the allure of the past, nothing is to be treasured so much as the here and now. It is to Soren, who graduates from kindergarten the very day I submit this manuscript, that I will dedicate this my second book.

1

RICHARD HOOKER: THE MYTH

"Hooker," it has been aptly said, "is the name of a book rather than the name of a man."[1] And it is true that there are few authors in the Western tradition who disappeared so completely into their writings, who encapsulated so perfectly the type of the quiet and unassuming scholar, shunning the public eye and content to throw his weight upon the wheel of history from the shelter of a candlelit study. Among the great names of his own era, many were known for their extraordinary learning, but are remembered so well in part for the very active role they took in the tumultuous affairs of the age. When we think of Luther and Calvin, Knox and Cranmer, these were men who, like the great prophets of Israel from whom they drew inspiration, preached before princes or corresponded with kings, and felt called "to pluck up and to break down, to destroy and to overthrow, to build and to plant" (Jer 1:10).

Not so Hooker. We are not sure that he ever even found himself in the presence of the monarch whom he so revered, Queen Elizabeth, nor did he even dare to formally

1. Morris, introduction to *Of the Laws of Ecclesiastical Polity*, I:v.

dedicate any of his books to her with an appropriately flattering introductory letter (a common practice in those days). Nor was he much interested in plucking up or breaking down; quite the contrary, nothing filled him so much with dismay as the seemingly contagious fashion for such "plucking up" that he saw in the Puritan reformers of this era. He wrote, in fact, quite expressly to preserve the church he knew and loved—if possible in being, if not, at least in memory, as the haunting first lines of his *Laws of Ecclesiastical Polity* express: "Though for no other cause, yet for this: that posterity may know we have not loosely through silence permitted things to pass away as in a dream, there shall be for men's information extant thus much concerning the present state of the Church of God established amongst us, and their careful endeavor *who* would have upheld the same" (I.1.1).

In saying that Hooker is the name of a book, not of a man, we also highlight the towering shadow of this magnum opus, the *Laws*, which has loomed so large as to often obscure his worthy and profound sermons and tractates (though these total just a few hundred pages). Calvin may be known by his *Institutes*, and Aquinas by his *Summa Theologiae*, but good Calvinists will turn also to the *Commentaries*, and good Thomists to the *Summa Contra Gentiles*. For Hooker, it is only the *Laws*, a volume that is a world unto itself. In it we find theology in abundance, in most of its various branches, liturgics, law, political theory, sociology, hermeneutics, metaphysics, epistemology, ethics, polemics and irenics, and more, all in a prose style that, as C. S. Lewis observed, "is, for its purpose, perhaps the most perfect in English."[2]

Hooker wrote in the 1590s, that high tide of Elizabethan intellectual and literary culture which defined the

---

2. *English Literature in the Sixteenth Century*, 462.

shape of our language and culture right down to the present. While Hooker was in London drafting his *Laws*, Shakespeare was just on the opposite bank of the Thames writing *The Taming of the Shrew* (which has some interesting thematic parallels with the *Laws*, actually),[3] and Spenser had just returned to Ireland after coming to London to publish and promote his *Faerie Queene*. Francis Bacon was a leading advisor at court, just beginning his literary career. Like these other men, the scale of Hooker's achievement looms up out of the relative mediocrity of his predecessors with a suddenness that can baffle the historian. Stanley Archer observes, "It is no more possible to account for Hooker's achievement than for those of Shakespeare and Milton, Spenser and Bacon."[4]

Yet before we pause to consider this achievement, this magnum opus, and even before we put some flesh and bones on it by considering Hooker the man, we must take seriously the four centuries that separate us from him; we must reckon with Hooker the myth.

HOOKER THE "ANGLICAN"

For Hooker, perhaps even more than most great writers of the past, it is difficult to disentangle the man and his book from his many interpreters and devotees. This may seem surprising at first, for while we all know of Augustinians, Thomists, Lutherans, and Calvinists, wearing their master's name as a badge of honor, there have been to date few, if any, self-styled Hookerians. Rather, they simply called themselves "Anglicans," and therein lies the problem, for there are perhaps as many definitions of what it means to be a good Anglican as there are Anglicans. But it is not hard

3. See Jacobsen, "Law of a Commonweal."
4. *Richard Hooker*, 1.

to see, from the description above, how the Anglican Communion, and particularly the Church of England during the heyday of Britishness—the eighteenth and nineteenth centuries—came to see Richard Hooker as summing up everything that it admired about itself: learned and bookish, quiet and unassuming in conversation, but with a penchant for drama and eloquence when it came to writing, dispositionally conservative and suspicious of innovation, restrained but earnest in piety and worship, moderate in doctrine, steeped in the classics and respectful of history but with a pragmatic eye for the needs of the present, principled but flexible, and very, very English.

Of course, within this broad picture there was quite enormous room for differences in churchmanship and politics, with those at every point on the broad "Anglican" spectrum—and some beyond it—claiming Hooker as inspiration. To tell the story of the various Hookers that have paraded through the pages of English history and theology over the past four centuries is, perhaps, to tell the story of the Church of England, and now the Anglican Communion, in all its permutations and conflicts.[5] During the early seventeenth century, Hooker could be admired and invoked by more evangelical and quasi-puritan churchmen, like James Ussher and Thomas Morton, and by high-churchmen like Lancelot Andrewes and Archbishop Laud. After the violent rift of the English Civil War, Hooker was claimed as the patron saint of the new high-church orthodoxy that dominated after the 1662 Act of Uniformity, but could at the same time be championed by the greatest Dissenting theologian of the era, Richard Baxter. As the great divide in English political theory opened up between the absolutist Robert Filmer and the liberal John Locke, both men invoked the authority

---

5. For Hooker's seventeenth-century reception, see Brydon, *Evolving Reputation*.

of the "judicious Mr. Hooker," and Edmund Burke, the so-called "Father of British Conservatism" was to do the same a century later, as were some of America's founding fathers. As the nineteenth-century Oxford Movement began their campaign for an English church that was more Catholic than Protestant, they managed to shoehorn Hooker into their movement as a somewhat unreliable standard-bearer, with Oxford Movement leader John Keble having to make a few apologies for Hooker's various Reformed indiscretions in his influential edition of Hooker's works.

As the chaos of the nineteenth century gave way to an uneasy truce for much of the twentieth, evangelical Anglican churchmen tended to retreat from positions of influence, leaving the field largely to a moderate and sometimes woolly Anglo-Catholicism which prided itself above all on being a *via media*—between which two extremes exactly, it was never quite sure. In such an environment, the reputation of Hooker thrived as never before, even as the influence of his writing somewhat paradoxically declined, so that Cargill Thompson could observe in 1972 that "Hooker has tended to fall into the category of thinkers who are more written about than *studied*,"[6] and Arthur Stanley, eleven years later, that "Richard Hooker belongs in that category of authors who are more honored than read."[7] As Anglican theological education has generally declined over recent decades, even this cannot be taken for granted, and Charles Miller, in a recent book on Hooker, and Stephen McGrade, in a new edition of the *Laws*, have professed their aspiration to bring Hooker back into the vicarage and the classroom.[8] Even among most Anglican scholars and writers of the late twentieth century, the concrete details of Hooker's writing

---

6. "Philosopher of the Politic Society," 132.
7. *Richard Hooker*, i.
8. See Miller, *Vision of God*, 11.

had been so thoroughly overshadowed by the many-layered myth of the judicious, *via media* Hooker that had grown up around them, that he could regularly be invoked as a paragon of Anglican "sweet reasonableness" over against the enemy of the moment (Calvinists and evangelicals being the two most likely parties), without so much as a citation or quotation being needed. Moreover, certain modern Anglican theological truisms, such as the idea that one ought not really draw a distinction between the visible and invisible church, for fear of demeaning the former, could simply be attributed to Hooker, in direct contradiction of his own statements on the subject.[9]

At least four elements make up the mythical Hooker as he commonly appeared until the last generation, and still does among a number of readers. First, this Hooker is a serene philosopher, floating high above the fray of petty party polemic as he penned his timeless theological tome. True, he was not your run-of-the-mill Elizabethan polemicist, but he does spend much of the *Laws* down in the trenches, so to speak, and knows how to hold his own in a war of words (see chapter 5 for a fuller discussion). Second, this Hooker is thoroughly anti-Calvinist, steering the English church away from the hot-headed and hard-hearted Genevan. True, he departs from Calvin's particular formulations on a number of issues, but then, so did almost any Reformed theologian of stature during this period; historians now recognize that Calvin was simply one Reformed authority among many in the sixteenth and seventeenth centuries. And this is, after all, Hooker's main point when he discusses Calvin in his Preface: "but wise men are men, and truth is truth" (Pref. 2.7). Calvin deserved honor, but not adulation, and certainly ought not become the yardstick of orthodoxy. Third, the

---

9. See for instance Miller, *Vision of God*, 228, and for more on this issue, ch. 10 below.

mythical Hooker is the great retriever of Thomas Aquinas, who had been rejected by his Protestant predecessors. It is certainly true that Hooker was a great admirer of Aquinas, and draws on him particularly in Book I of the *Laws*, but there was nothing particularly novel about this among later sixteenth-century Protestants. Hooker's Reformed contemporary at the University of Leiden, Franciscus Junius, draws upon Aquinas far *more* extensively in his own treatise on law.[10] Finally, this Hooker is a "high-churchman," a defender of rich liturgy, tradition, episcopacy, sacraments, and all those wonderful things with a faint whiff of incense that people like about Anglicanism. True enough, he does defend all those things, but the anachronistic metaphor of height does little to help us understand in what sense or for what reasons he defends each. In fact, much of what he has to say on each would make later Anglican high-churchmen uncomfortable, at least if they were reading him carefully. He is certainly no low-church evangelical either, however, but we will have to wait till chapters 10 and 11 before attempting to properly map out his ecclesiology.

HOOKER IN RECENT SCHOLARSHIP

Thankfully, even as the effacement of the real Hooker and the real *Laws* was reaching its apogee, a contrary trend began to take shape, which has revolutionized Hooker scholarship over the past quarter century. Or rather, two contrary trends, each contrary to the received myth of Hooker, but equally contrary to one another, began to take shape. They may both be conveniently dated to 1988, when Peter Lake, the great historian of Puritanism and early modern England, published his book *Anglicans and Puritans?* and

---

10. See my forthcoming "Hooker, Junius, and a Reformed Theology of Law."

Torrance Kirby, now a leading Reformation scholar, defended his Oxford dissertation, soon afterward published as *Richard Hooker's Doctrine of the Royal Supremacy*.

Both were historians above all, out to puncture unhistorical hagiographic versions of Richard Hooker, but with very different methods and agendas. Kirby, relying on a close reading of Hooker's text and earlier Reformation theologians such as Luther and Calvin, came to the following conclusions:

1. Hooker self-consciously presented himself not as the paradigmatic "Anglican," the guardian of the *via media* understood as not quite Protestant or Catholic, but simply as an English Reformed theologian, representative of the best of what his Protestant predecessors had to offer.

2. Indeed, not only this, but Hooker went so far as to accuse his Puritan opponents of being bad Protestants, unwittingly eroding some key gains of the Reformation.

3. Hooker was, it would appear, by and large correct in this self-presentation.

To some extent, Kirby's arguments had been anticipated by many of the best readers of Hooker over the previous decades and centuries, though they had never been stated so crisply and compellingly (and point 2, in particular, had been little noticed by most).

Kirby's argument obviously threatened to dismantle the comfortable myths that supported much contemporary moderate and liberal Anglicanism, inasmuch as it aligned Hooker much more closely with that bête noire of modernity, John Calvin. Perhaps Hooker was not so much the apostle of reason over Scripture, of open-ended open-mindedness over doctrinal clarity, of historical change over timeless truth that many had happily imagined. Perhaps he hewed too close for comfort to unpopular Protestant doctrines like *sola Scriptura*, predestination, a spiritual presence in the Eucharist, the visible/invisible church distinction, the Christian magistrate, etc. It should be little surprise, then, that some evangelical Anglicans latched onto Kirby's reading as a way to claim Hooker's great mantle for themselves in the bitter debates currently tearing at the fabric of the Anglican Communion.[11] In response, their more liberal counterparts sought to smear Kirby as a partisan ideologue abusing Hooker for a contemporary ecclesiastical agenda.[12] History, it would appear, is never just history, but always the scaffolding for some contemporary project or another; shake the scaffold, and you shouldn't be surprised if those on top start lobbing stones down at you.

The other new trend in Hooker interpretation, represented by Peter Lake and his disciples, was very different indeed, and characterized perhaps above all by its attempt to avoid any sign of ecclesiastical partisanship. To be sure, it in fact shared with Kirby the first plank of his argument—that Hooker did in fact represent himself as authentically Reformed—but it firmly rejected the third—i.e., that he actually was. This was in part due to a methodological commitment to agnosticism about any such truth-claims; as Lake summarized this historiographical orthodoxy, "The aim is to describe and to understand, not to adjudicate these disputes."[13] From this socio-rhetorical point of view, if both Hooker and his Puritan interlocutors claim to be most faithful to the Reformers, the historian simply has no

11. See for instance Atkinson, *Richard Hooker*, and the preface by Alister McGrath.

12. See for instance Gibbs, "Prophet of Anglicanism." This smear is the more baffling given that Kirby is not, in fact, an evangelical.

13. Lake, "Puritanism, Arminianism, and Nicholas Tyacke," 12.

business adjudicating this particular debate. The most he can do is say what factors (which are as likely to be social and political as they are intellectual) led each party to make this claim.

Somewhat oddly, though, this is not really what we find Lake himself doing in *Anglicans and Puritans* or subsequent writings; he is not content to tell us what Hooker said he thought, but to analyze what he *really* thought, and whether it was in fact faithful to his predecessors or something new. Lake is convinced that by attending carefully to the political context of these writings and customary rhetorical conventions, we can read through the superficial "politically correct" affirmations in Hooker's text and detect a sometimes very different subtext, staking out new theological ground on issues like the doctrine of Scripture, political authority, ecclesiology, the sacraments, predestination, and much more. On this basis, Lake concludes that although it is clearly not the case that Hooker was the paragon of some already-existing *via media* "Anglicanism," as many forms of the mythology had it, he could very well be said to be the forerunner of it, or its surreptitious "inventor."[14] This claim of Lake's—that on a whole host of topics, Hooker "invented" a new theological synthesis—has proven remarkably influential, despite the fact that it would seem to fly in the face of Lake's own methodological agnosticism, and despite the fact that Lake has never really claimed any expertise on any Protestant theology beyond England's shores.

It should be clear from this description that while both trends puncture the old myth of the serene *via media* Hooker, they do so at very different points. Kirby's interpretation challenges the theology of the received Hooker, insisting that it is less distinctively "Anglican" (whatever

14. *Anglicans and Puritans*, 227.

that might mean) than simply English Reformed. Lake challenges the rhetoric and method of the received Hooker, insisting that he is not a detached irenical philosopher, but a pugilistic polemicist willing to talk out of both sides of his mouth, who must be read with a hermeneutic of suspicion to be rightly understood. Despite this, however, many Anglicans who have had a heavy stake in the old moderate progressive Hooker have been willing to accept Lake's hermeneutic of suspicion as the necessary price to pay to ward off Kirby's more evangelical interpretation.[15] Meanwhile, many scholars in the humanities, with little theological interest, have gravitated toward Lake's approach as one well representing the emphases on socio-political context, and deconstructive rhetorical analysis, that dominate the historical discipline today.[16]

Curiously, though, while in most respects decrying earlier readings of Hooker as un-historical, this school of interpretation has at one point remained largely enslaved to the biases of the older Anglican Hooker: its insularity. The old urban legend of the London newspaper headline that read "Fog in Channel, Continent Cut Off" says it all: Brits have always had a tendency to think of whatever happens in continental Europe as a largely irrelevant sideshow that has little impact on the important, and very distinctively British, goings-on within the British Isles. The old myth of the oh-so-Anglican Hooker had as one of its key pillars

---

15. One can witness this in A. J. Joyce's *Richard Hooker and Anglican Moral Theology*, where she appeals to Lake's method of "historical objectivity" and adopts a deconstructive reading of his rhetoric expressly in order to refute the evangelicals like Kirby and even, it sometimes feels, to render Hooker more appealing to modern Anglican sensibilities.

16. Ethan Shagan's treatment of Hooker in ch. 3 of the *Rule of Moderation*, with its explicit appeal to Foucauldian method, is perhaps one of the striking examples of this approach.

the idea that while Lutherans could have their Luther and Calvinists their Calvin, Englishmen had their Hooker, and their other home-grown theologians, and so had no need to look abroad. It is a strange feature of some newer, more historically rigorous readings of Hooker that they remain shackled to this Anglo-centric perspective, especially as Reformation scholarship generally has taken a more and more international approach, recognizing the extraordinary cross-pollination between regions and traditions that characterized the sixteenth century. One strength of Kirby's approach, and other scholars who have followed in his footsteps, is his close attention to the role of the Continental Reformed theologians Peter Martyr Vermigli and Heinrich Bullinger in the development of the Elizabethan Church and perhaps Richard Hooker particularly. Recent work has widened the lens to consider the relevance of figures like Philipp Melanchthon, Jerome Zanchi, and Franciscus Junius as well for grasping Hooker's theological milieu.[17]

From all this, I hope it is evident by now that Richard Hooker is of profound relevance, and ought to be of profound interest, to more than just Anglicans. If Kirby is right, then Protestants of any stripe have a great deal to learn from Hooker. He was in many ways a faithful exponent of some of Luther's key ideas, whose work is partially parallelled by eminent early modern Lutheran jurists. He was deeply conversant with the theology of the great leaders of the Reformed tradition, such as Bullinger, Vermigli, and Calvin, and although not slavishly devoted to any of these, saw himself, as almost every English Protestant theologian of his day, as part of the international family of Reformed churches. The painful later rift between "Reformed" and

---

17. See the forthcoming Kindred-Barnes and Littlejohn, eds., *Richard Hooker and Reformed Orthodoxy*, for a collection of essays trying to situate Hooker within this broader context.

"Anglican," which has had such harmful consequences for both traditions, was still many decades in the future. And to the extent that Hooker was not a man for party labels, but interested simply in being a "reformed catholic," a Protestant steeped in the tradition of the Fathers and scholastics, he ought to hold great interest for ecumenically-minded Protestants of all traditions, and indeed ecumenically-minded Catholics as well.

Even if Lake is right, and some of the above points turn out to be overstated, then Hooker ought to hold wide interest for political theorists and ethicists, not to mention sociologists of religion. With a burst of renewed interest in Christian ethics and political theology in recent years, especially in North America, many Protestants have felt like they've had to show up to the party empty-handed. Where Catholics have Aquinas and the comprehensive documents of Catholic Social Teaching, Protestants are often unsure where to turn to in finding a robust foundation for ethical and political reasoning in our tradition. Although in this slim volume, I can do no more than hint at some of the reasons why, I believe that we will find few if any better resources for such reasoning, from the age of Reformation at least, than the thought of Richard Hooker. I must, however, postpone any further reflections on what Richard Hooker might have to offer us today until we come to the final chapter.

In parts 2 and 3 we will delve much more deeply into the vision that drove Hooker's theology, and the nuanced ways he sought to engage some of the controversial questions of his age. But first, we must say a bit more about the tumultuous age into which Hooker was born, and how he came to find himself an apologist for "the present state of the Church of God established" in Elizabethan England.

FOR DISCUSSION

1. What are some reasons why Hooker's thought has come to mean so many different things to different people?
2. Compare and contrast the recent interpretations of Hooker offered by Torrance Kirby and Peter Lake.

2

RICHARD HOOKER: THE MAN

IN ITSELF, THE LIFE of Richard Hooker is perhaps remarkable above all for its unremarkableness. As mentioned already, his was much more the contemplative than the active life, unlike the thunderous movers and shakers of the first decades of the Reformation, and equally unlike some of his more hot-headed Puritan opponents in England. His famous controversy with presbyterian leader Walter Travers at the Temple (about which there is more below), is perhaps so well-known and frequently-discussed chiefly because it was Hooker's only notable moment of public conflict during a time and place when public conflict seemed more the norm than the exception for many churchmen.

Nor did Hooker ever hold any particularly high office, neither bishopric nor deanery, nor a mastership at one of the great colleges of Cambridge or Oxford. In this he was virtually unique among the leading English theological writers of his time, especially those who took up their pen on behalf of the established church, who could generally expect swift promotion into and perhaps within the ranks of the twenty-seven bishops of Elizabeth's church. This lack of promotion may owe something to Hooker's relatively early death at forty-six, though younger consecrations were not uncommon. But it also seems that Hooker had no strong desire for high ecclesiastical office, requesting to be transferred from his influential post at the Temple to a rural parish in 1591. Indeed, whatever criticisms his opponents then and now have had for him, none have ever been able to accuse him of using theological polemic as a tool for personal ambition.

On account of this relatively quiet life, we have for Hooker even less biographical information than for many in this era (and as Shakespeare scholars well know, that isn't much even for the most well-known figures). Our chief resource is the 1665 biography by Izaak Walton, often mocked for its dubious anecdotes and unabashedly hagiographical tone. However, in Walton's defense, subsequent biographical research, and the study of Hooker's texts, has uncovered little to contradict Walton's flattering portrait of a man characterized chiefly by humility, piety, charity, and extraordinary learning. Indeed, one of Hooker's friends, John Spenser, wrote shortly after Hooker's death,

> What admirable height of learning and depth of judgment dwelled in the lowly mind of this true humble man, great in all wise men's eyes, except his own; with what gravity and majesty of speech, his tongue and pen uttered heavenly mysteries, whose eyes in the humility of his heart were always cast down to the ground; how all things that proceeded from him were breathed, as from the spirit of love, as if he like the bird of the Holy Ghost, the dove, had wanted gall; let those who knew him not in person judge by . . . his writings.[1]

---

1. Keble, ed., *Works*, 1:152–53.

Modern scholars have been inclined to raise an eyebrow or two at this halo-tinged description, not least because they have taken Spenser's advice and looked more closely at Hooker's writings. In particular, we now have access to his handwritten marginal notes in response to the one published criticism of his writings to appear in his lifetime, *A Christian Letter of Certain English Protestants* (1599). They range from the mildly snarky "A doctrine which would have pleased Caligula, Nero, and other such monsters to hear," to the obviously ill-tempered "Ignorant ass!" to the frankly hilarious, "Your godfathers and godmothers have much to answer unto God for not seeing you better catechised."[2] Many modern scholars have taken these as evidence that Hooker was only mild-mannered and charitable until poked; then he could react with as much ire as anyone. However, C. S. Lewis has observed that in fact what these marginal notes tell us is how hard Hooker worked to discipline his personal emotions (which were not always saintlike) to keep them from distorting his public discourse.[3] For we also have access to the incomplete manuscript of Hooker's response to the *Christian Letter* which he intended for publication, and in this there is no trace of the rancour or personal insults which come through in the private notes. This stands in notable contrast to the typical conventions of sixteenth-century theological polemic, even (perhaps especially) among such Protestant heroes as Luther or Calvin.

---

2. *FLE* 4:13, 22.

3. *English Literature in the Sixteenth Century*, 453: "The mellow gold of the *Polity* is not merely the natural overflow of a mild eupeptic who has good reason to be pleased with the status quo. It is the work of prudence, of art, of moral virtue, and (as Hooker would no doubt have said) of Grace. It is also an obedience to 'decorum.'"

Of course, this does not at all mean that Hooker could not be moved to strong passions at what he saw to be in error, nor that the grand prose of the *Laws* is free from passages of fairly sharp polemic or cutting backhanded compliments. But all this shows is that Hooker cared deeply about the truths at stake. Although a number of recent scholars have sought to accuse him of deliberate and slanderous misrepresentation of his opponents, thus far they have failed to substantiate their charges with much evidence.[4] We will have much more to say about this when we come to chapter 5, on Hooker as polemicist. For now, though, let us survey what we do know about Hooker's life, and perhaps more importantly, situate it against the backdrop of tempestuous events and theological wranglings that characterized this formative period in English history.

EARLY LIFE

Richard Hooker was born in late 1553 or early 1554 in a village on the outskirts of Exeter in southwest England, then, as now, a prosperous port and a cathedral city. Hooker's immediate family, despite some notable ancestors, were not particularly prosperous, and his father Roger appears to have spent most of Hooker's childhood abroad in Ireland as a soldier and adventurer. This left young Richard and his mother dependent upon his uncle John, perhaps fortunately for Richard and for posterity, since John was not merely well-to-do but well-educated and well-connected. In 1554, though, these connections—notably to the great Italian reformer Peter Martyr Vermigli, who had been serving as

---

4. See for instance Joyce, *Richard Hooker and Anglican Moral Theology*, ch. 3, and my remarks in "Search for a Reformed Hooker," 76–78. Of course, this does not mean that he is never guilty of uncharitable reading, nor of seeking to put his opponents in a bad light, but these are rather different charges. See further chapter 5 below.

professor of divinity at Oxford under the Protestant king Edward VI—must have felt like more curse than blessing. Queen Mary (known to history not unreasonably as "Bloody Mary" for her martyrdom of hundreds of Protestants) had just ascended the throne on the boy-king's death, and was determined to reverse the rapid progress the Reformation had made in England over the past few years. Vermigli and other foreign Protestant leaders who had been invited over by Edward were allowed to pack their bags and return to the Continent, and in the chaotic first few months of Mary's reign, many of their friends and students hastened to join them. These included John Hooker and Vermigli's star student, John Jewel, who was also to play a significant role in the young Richard's life. Those Protestants who already held high office in the Church of England were not so fortunate; they remained at their posts, were arrested, and before long burned at the stake: most notable among them were Bishop John Hooper on February 9, 1555, Bishops Nicholas Ridley and Hugh Latimer on October 16 of that year, and Archbishop Thomas Cranmer on March 21 of the following year.

Fortunately for the Hooker family, the Protestant cause did not have to wait long for a dramatic change of fortunes. The sudden death of Mary in late 1558 and accession of the firmly Protestant Queen Elizabeth struck contemporary Protestants as a great act of divine deliverance, and it is difficult for us looking back, and seeing the profound ambiguity of Elizabeth's policies, to understand just how fervently many of her Protestant subjects reverenced her. Hooker himself would later write of her, having lived virtually his whole life under her extraordinarily long reign, as

> her especially whose sacred power matched with incomparable goodness of nature has hitherto been God's most happy instrument by him miraculously kept for works of so miraculous

> preservation and safety to others, that as "By the sword of God and Gideon," was sometime the cry of the people Israel, so it might deservedly be at this day the joyful song of innumerable multitudes, yea the Emblem of some estates and Dominions in the world, and (which must be eternally confessed even with tears of thankfulness) the true inscription style or title of all Churches as yet standing within this Realm, "By the goodness of God and his servant Elizabeth we are" (Book V, Dedication.10).

Elizabeth's accession brought the exiled English Protestants such as John Jewel and John Hooker hastening home. As she rapidly moved to institutionalize England's third great religious change in barely a decade, many of these exiles took up positions as bishops in her church, ensuring the profound ongoing influence of Vermigli and also Heinrich Bullinger, the leader of the Reformed church at Zurich where many of these exiles had resided.

John Hooker, meanwhile, returned to Exeter, where within a few years he noticed the precocious talents of his nephew Richard, and funded his education at the local grammar school. By 1568 or 1569, Richard was deemed ready for further study at university, a privilege reserved for just a handful in his day. To financially support his studies, John Hooker turned to his old friend John Jewel, now installed as bishop of nearby Salisbury and the leading apologist of the Church of England. Jewel interviewed Richard, was deeply impressed by his talents, and agreed to secure him a place at his own alma mater, Corpus Christi College at Oxford, provide financial support, and keep an eye on Richard's developing career.

When Hooker came to Oxford, portentous developments were beginning to unfold at her more radical rival, Cambridge University. There a young theology lecturer named Thomas Cartwright was lecturing through the book of Acts, and expounding a new theory of church government that came to be known as presbyterianism.[5] It appears that Cartwright got some of his ideas from his studies in Geneva with Calvin's successor Theodore Beza, some perhaps from the structure of the independent churches of foreign exiles in London, and some from the Scottish church and his friend there Andrew Melville. But most of all, Cartwright claimed to get it direct from Scripture, finding there in the text a detailed biblical blueprint for church polity which no one had recognized there since the first generations after Christ. Cartwright was soon to make enough enemies, by his teaching and his personality, to get dismissed from his post at Cambridge, but he had gained enough adherents to start a movement. The presbyterian theory was quick to gain credibility among England's more zealous and restless Protestants, who were seething with disgruntlement at the bishops after the recent "Vestiarian Controversy."

This had started when a number of Protestant clergy, generally those who had been exiled abroad under Mary, declined to wear the ceremonial vestments stipulated in Elizabeth's new church order, since they seemed to symbolize too much continuity with the very recent Catholic past. Elizabeth, appreciating ceremony, not liking to be contradicted, and trying to maintain delicate diplomatic relations with Catholic monarchs abroad (not to mention with her many Catholic subjects still in England), clamped down and demanded complete uniformity. Her bishops dutifully though regretfully enforced her orders, leading the scrupulous dissenters to appeal to Reformers abroad. These by and large sided with the bishops, not necessarily out of support

---

5. The best studies of Cartwright and his ecclesiology are perhaps still the venerable old treatments by A. F. Scott Pearson: *Church and State*, and *Thomas Cartwright and Elizabethan Puritanism*. See also Joan Lockwood O'Donovan, *Theology of Law and Authority*, ch. 8.

for the vestments per se, but out of support for the right of the monarch to establish uniform standards in such secondary matters, or *adiaphora* as they were called. Some of the English Protestants, however, were not so sure. Perhaps no human authority had the right to meddle with liturgical matters, which must instead be guided by Scripture. Perhaps even, as Cartwright had begun to argue, church government too fell within the realm of things laid down unchangeably in Scripture.

Unfortunately for such reform-minded Protestants, the political atmosphere was increasingly unfavorable for such concerns. In 1569, Catholic nobles in the north of England had rebelled against Elizabeth, and the pope responded belatedly by issuing a bull excommunicating her and calling on her subjects to rebel. Protestants who questioned her authority over the church were bound to look bad, and many churchmen had difficulty sympathizing with their agitations when they ought to be united against the common enemy of Rome. Nevertheless, some of Cartwright's younger and more radical disciples pressed ahead, releasing an *Admonition to Parliament* just before Parliament met in 1572, which brazenly declared, "We in England are so far off from having a church rightly reformed, according to the prescript of God's word, that as yet we are not come to the outward face of the same,"[6] and called for the establishment of presbyterian government, along with other major reforms. The pamphlet was suppressed by the authorities, but still traveled far and wide, creating a sensation.[7] A tedious but heated literary battle ensued over the following five years between Cartwright (now in exile

---

6. Frere and Douglas, eds., *Puritan Manifestoes*, 9.

7. The classic study of the rise of the Puritan movement, including the Admonition controversy, remains Patrick Collinson's *Elizabethan Puritan Movement*.

in Holland) and John Whitgift, Master of Trinity College, Cambridge, and the future Archbishop of Canterbury. Despite the frequently trivial nature of the issues (for instance, where in the church the minister should stand at certain points in the service), profound differences in ecclesiology lay under the surface, and the interaction generated heated polemics, especially from the younger Cartwright. Hooker was later to refer obliquely to Cartwright with one of his most famous lines in the *Laws*: "Concerning the defender of which admonitions, all that I mean to say is but this: There will come a time when three words uttered with charity and meekness shall receive a far more blessed reward than three thousand volumes written with disdainful sharpness of wit" (Pref. 2.10). Indeed, many scholars have suggested that the *Laws* was written in part as a response to Cartwright's last salvo in the controversy, which Whitgift had never bothered to answer. But let us get back to Hooker at Oxford.

Despite the controversies raging throughout the 1570s, this was for Hooker himself a time of quiet and relatively uneventful study. He came under the wing of some of the best theological minds at Oxford, with William Cole as president of his college, John Rainolds as his primary tutor, and Lawrence Humphrey as another teacher and mentor. All three had been exiles under Mary and disciples of Peter Martyr Vermigli, and all three had moderate Puritan sympathies of one kind or another. Humphrey had been one of the instigators in the earlier Vestiarian controversy, though he did not continue the battle when it was clear it had gone against him. John Rainolds, esteemed as one of the most learned Englishmen of his age, was later to serve as one of the Puritan delegates to the Hampton Court Conference of 1604, where King James considered Puritan objections to the Book of Common Prayer. The scattered evidence we have suggests that these men seem to have imparted some of their moderate Puritan influence on Hooker during his years of study, and he remained lifelong friends with Rainolds. This evidence lends credence to his insistence, at the beginning of the *Laws*, that he started out sympathetic to the Puritan cause, and even where he did not understand all of their contentions, he assumed they must be well-grounded, until he turned to investigate carefully for himself. Perhaps a more lasting influence on Hooker's thought was Humphrey's and Rainolds's appreciation for Aristotle, of whose works their teacher Vermigli had been an enthusiastic advocate. To be sure, most educated Reformed theologians of this period would have been well-versed in the Aristotelian system, but the philosopher left a particularly deep impression on Hooker, which manifests itself frequently in the pages of the *Laws*.

In any case, his academic career progressed as well as might be expected, with Hooker gaining his BA in 1573, his MA in 1577, and becoming a fellow of the college in 1579. He also began to tutor his own students, beginning quite auspiciously with Edwin Sandys and George Cranmer. Edwin's father, also named Edwin, was a friend of Jewel's, *another* Vermigli disciple, and currently bishop of London. He was soon to become Archbishop of York, the second-ranking churchman in the kingdom. George, as his last name suggests, was related to Thomas Cranmer, the late Archbishop of Canterbury. Both students were to become Hooker's lifelong friends and advocates, and Edwin had an illustrious career in Parliament and as a member of the Virginia Company.

PUBLIC CONTROVERSIES

By the time the 1580s began, Hooker was being encouraged by his mentors to take a more active part in church affairs. He was ordained a deacon in 1579 and a priest in 1581, and shortly afterward was given an opportunity to preach at Paul's Cross, the great public pulpit by St. Paul's Cathedral where aspiring preachers could expect to have many of the great men and women of London, including sometimes the queen herself, among their audience. Never one to make things too easy for himself, he chose as his topic the doctrine of predestination, offering, as it would appear from the accounts we have, a moderate version of the doctrine closer to that taught by Heinrich Bullinger of Zurich than to Calvin and Beza's stronger doctrine, which was then coming increasingly into vogue.[8] Predestination and controversy have always gone hand-in-hand, and Hooker quickly encountered his fair share of detractors, although, since John Aylmer, Bishop of London, appears to have supported him, it turned out well enough for him in the end. During this first stay in London, Hooker also appears to have perhaps first made the acquaintance of John Churchman, who was to serve as a landlord, patron, and eventually father-in-law in the coming years.

A little over three years later, in early 1585, Hooker's well-positioned friends secured for him the nomination to the prestigious position of Master of the Temple. The Temple Church, so named because it founded by the Knights Templar in the late twelfth century, and built as a small-scale replica of the Church of the Holy Sepulchre in Jerusalem, which served as the parish of the lawyers and law students of the Inner and Middle Temple. As the heart of the legal profession in England, the Temple was a position of substantial influence and political importance, and Hooker's appointment to such a position at the age of just thirty-one tells us something about how well he had

---

8. See Neelands, "Richard Hooker's Paul's Cross Sermon."

impressed his superiors. However, there was also a fair bit of political wrangling that lay behind the decision.

After several years of relative quiet, the presbyterian movement had burst back onto the scene in the early 1580s. John Whitgift, once appointed Archbishop of Canterbury in 1583, moved quickly to enforce strict conformity on the Church of England, as Elizabeth seems to have intended in selecting him for the position. By requiring Puritan-minded ministers to subscribe unreservedly to the Thirty-Nine Articles and Book of Common Prayer, he hoped to weed out conscientious objectors. Instead, he provoked a backlash. Beleaguered ministers quickly appealed to sympathetic nobleman to push for reforms in Parliament, and in the meantime, gravitated toward the more radical presbyterian wing, seeing a complete overhaul of the church as the only way to attain their aims. By 1584, a secret presbyterian network was taking shape throughout the country, and it would grow and consolidate over the next five years.

Walter Travers, one of the leading presbyterian theorists, who had not even been ordained in the Church of England, had enough powerful friends to secure a position as Reader (i.e., assistant minister) in the Temple Church back in 1581, and with the retirement of the aged Master, was expected to succeed him. However, in the increasingly polarized climate, Whitgift and Aylmer intervened to select a more suitable candidate. Travers had already succeeded in swaying many of the members of the Temple to a Puritan and even presbyterian perspective, so Hooker was selected as a middle-of-the-road candidate who would hopefully be acceptable to the parishioners, and to Travers, to whom he was related by marriage, but reliable from the standpoint of the authorities.

Conflict began almost immediately, however. Travers had already gone some ways towards reorganizing the church along quasi-presbyterian lines, and he asked Hooker to wait for the congregation to formally approve his appointment to the post before taking up his ministry (since, for Travers, congregational approval was essential for a legitimate ministerial call). Hooker was bewildered by such a violation of protocol, and declined. After this inauspicious start, Travers treated Hooker's ministry with suspicion, never really conceding the authority of this government appointee five years his junior.

So it was not long before the tension exploded into a public confrontation. Later that year, Hooker preached a series of sermons on justification, in which he argued that, though the Catholic *doctrine* may be contrary to the gospel, that does not imply that all the Catholic faithful, holding that doctrine in confused form, are damned. Travers, hearing of the contents of the first sermon, decided to denounce it in his afternoon sermon, without conferring with Hooker first to be sure he had understood him properly. This unseemly spectacle continued for the next few weeks, with Hooker preaching each Sunday morning to a packed audience, and the crowds returning in the afternoon to hear Travers' refutation. Archbishop Whitgift, hearing of the proceedings, issued an order silencing Travers, upon which Travers appealed his case to the Queen's Privy Council, denouncing Hooker for various breaches of orthodoxy. The council found in favor of Hooker, however, and Travers was dismissed from his post. Hooker, however, found his position at the Temple quite uncomfortable thereafter, with many of his parishioners sympathetic to their banished Reader, and he eagerly accepted transfer to a less prestigious rural parish in 1591.

During these same years, the presbyterian agitation was coming to a head in a series of high-stakes showdowns. Ever-bolder demands in Parliament were met with ever-more peremptory commands from the queen for Parliament to desist from discussing church policy; this, she said, was to be determined by the bishops, by which she meant primarily herself. Puritan ire, however, fell almost solely on the bishops, due to the profound personal loyalty to the queen which even the staunchest Puritans seem to have shared. In 1588 and 1589, a series of scurrilous tracts directed at the bishops and the leading conformist writers issued from the pen of an anonymous satirist named Martin Marprelate. So shocking was the tone of these pamphlets that Cartwright, Travers, and other leaders rushed to condemn them, but the damage was done. Counter-propagandists and court preachers were quickly able to begin turning the public relations tide. In this they were helped also by the seemingly miraculous defeat of the Spanish Armada that year, which seemed to manifest God's favor toward the English Church, and by drastically reducing the Catholic threat, enabled the government to focus their attention on the presbyterians as the leading public enemy.

The most radical reformers made the government's job comparatively easy. Several leaders defected from the presbyterian wing of reform to argue for some form of congregationalism, and the end of a nationally-established church altogether, which sounded little better than treason to most people's ears in 1590. Still worse, a fanatic by the name of William Hacket claimed to be anointed by the Holy Ghost to bring judgment upon the queen and the whole English church. After attracting a few followers and inciting a riot, he was arrested and executed for treason. The ecclesiastical authorities had little difficulty convincing themselves and others that this sort of fanaticism was the logical result of the biblicism and misplaced zeal of the presbyterian reformers. Cartwright and other leaders were brought to trial, and although most were released, they got

WRITING THE *LAWS*

In the midst of all this, Hooker had conceived the idea for a book, a book systematically defending the worship and structure of the English church against her detractors. To be sure, such books, often funded by Whitgift or the court, were pouring from London's presses during these years, but Hooker wanted to try to do something different. Rather than simply answering the latest Puritan polemic in a tedious counterpoint, or composing a ponderous admonition to shut up and obey, as many conformists were doing, he wanted to write a systematic investigation of the whole debate, beginning with the foundational theological and hermeneutical questions at stake, and then gradually proceeding to the particular points of dispute. We are not quite sure when Hooker began work on the *Laws*, but it was perhaps not long after he married Joan Churchman in 1588, an auspicious union that brought him the support of a sympathetic father-in-law, a handsome dowry, and four children (though his two sons died in childhood). Unfortunately, like many writers who insist on doing things properly, rather than rushing their books to press, Hooker missed his moment. As he was wrapping up the first four books of an envisioned eight in 1592, the presbyterian movement was collapsing after the Hacket conspiracy and the trials. Suddenly, nobody seemed much interested in printing yet another contribution to the debate, especially one that spent more time talking about the eternal law than the threat of sedition.

Hooker's friend and former student Edwin Sandys came to his aid and financed the publication of the first four books, which received a lukewarm reception. Undeterred, Hooker pressed on with the monumental Book V, larger than the first four combined, which came to press in 1597. By this time, Hooker was residing at the prosperous parish of Bishopsbourne, near Canterbury, and had begun to establish a remarkable circle of friends. His closest appears to have been Hadrian Saravia, a Dutch theologian who had immigrated to England after ecclesiastical controversy at home and had turned his pen against the evils of presbyterianism, as he had seen it in Holland and now in England; no less a theologian than Theodore Beza, Calvin's successor at Geneva, was to take up the controversy with Saravia. Others included Lancelot Andrewes, the future favorite of James I and legendarily learned supervisor of the King James Bible, and Thomas Morton, who was to become one of the finest evangelical bishops in James's church a couple decades later.

Hooker's efforts to whip Books VI–VIII into satisfactory shape were slowed by constructive criticism from his friends, by the political sensitivity of the issues, and Hooker's idiosyncratic views on them (his theory of the royal supremacy might have scandalized his queen), and by the publication of *A Christian Letter* in 1599. Hooker spent some time composing a response to the criticisms of his work given there, which survives as the tantalizing "Dublin Fragments" (the manuscript having been discovered in the archive of Trinity College, Dublin), most of which focuses on the issue of predestination, and which has given rise to many rival readings of Hooker's doctrine. Unfortunately, as was all too common in those days, he fell ill from a cold which steadily worsened, and passed away on October 26, 1600, at the age of forty-six, leaving both this response and the *Laws* unfinished. Although his friends intended to bring these remaining writings to print in some form, it was not until 1648 that Books VI and VIII appeared, not until 1662 that Book VII appeared, and not until a few decades ago that scholars satisfactorily established that these volumes, as they have come down to us, are essentially genuine.

Less than three years after Hooker's death, his beloved queen passed away, followed within a few months by her dutiful archbishop, John Whitgift. This sudden changing of the guard, with James VI and I taking up his seat in London and Richard Bancroft at Canterbury, led to important changes in the policy of the English church, many of them in directions which Hooker himself had argued for. Although comparatively forgotten in the years immediately following his death, Hooker's reputation grew steadily throughout the century, until he attained the legendary status described in the last chapter.

So now it is time to turn our full attention to the book that nourished that legend, and on which Hooker expended fully a quarter of his life, the *Laws of Ecclesiastical Polity*.

FOR DISCUSSION

1. Who were some key influences on Hooker's early life and education, and how did they shape his thinking?
2. What factors led to the rise of the presbyterian movement in Elizabeth's reign, and why was it so controversial?
3. In what ways was Hooker's life unusual compared to that of other leading apologists for Elizabeth's church?

3

RICHARD HOOKER: THE BOOK

AMONG THE MORE FANCIFUL and yet irresistible stories which Hooker's biographer Izaak Walton recounts is one of Pope Clement VII, Hooker's contemporary and an implacable foe of Protestants. Upon reading the first portion of Hooker's *Laws*, Clement is supposed to have exclaimed, "There is no learning that this man hath not searched into; nothing too hard for his understanding: this man indeed deserves the name of an author; his books will get reverence by age, for there is in them such seeds of eternity, that if the rest be like this, they shall last till the last fire shall consume all learning."[1] Despite meeting with fairly uniform scholarly mistrust, this quotation continues to be repeated right down to the present, and as you can see, I can't resist repeating it myself. It gives Hooker a very ecumenical flavor, of course, but the quote is also wonderfully apt. Its "seeds of eternity" are indeed what captivates so many readers of the book today, just as they are what bewildered so many of its first readers.

---

1. Keble, ed., *Works*, I:90.

Richard Hooker: The Book

We have noted already that, for all his close engagement with his polemical context, Hooker clearly has an eye to posterity throughout the *Laws*—"that posterity may know we have not loosely through silence permitted things to pass away as in a dream" (Pref. 1.1)—and it is his extraordinarily skillful interweaving of these two contexts, the eternal and the temporal, that makes Hooker's *Laws* such a unique and fascinating work. You can never read more than a few pages without being reminded that Hooker has a very specific set of flesh-and-blood opponents in mind, and a very specific set of real-world institutions he wants to defend. And yet you can be forgiven for forgetting this on occasion, as Hooker over and over pulls back from the quarreling characters in the foreground to reveal the wide-angle theological and historical landscape, to the extent that portions of the work feel not unlike a systematic theology. Particularly notable examples are Hooker's systematic exposition of the various forms of law—eternal, celestial, natural, human, and divine—in Book I, or the remarkable *précis* of Christological orthodoxy in the middle of Book V, or the ecstatic discourse on the Eucharist a bit further on. While much modern scholarship has done well to remind us that Hooker's work is firmly rooted in the polemical soil of late Elizabethan England, only the most cynical reader can ignore these seeds of eternity scattered through it.

It is perhaps too easy for us, at four centuries' distance, to take for granted this fusion of the polemical and dogmatic horizons. And yet as C. S. Lewis aptly notes, it constituted "a revolution in the art of controversy," at least as that art had been practiced in English theology.

> Hitherto, in England, that art had involved only tactics; Hooker added strategy. Long before the close fighting in Book III begins, the Puritan position has been rendered desperate by the great

> flanking movements in Books I and II. . . . And all this, though excellent strategy, never strikes us as merely strategical. Truths unfold themselves, quietly and in due order, as if Hooker were developing—nay, we are sure that he is developing—his own philosophy for its own sake. . . .Thus the refutation of the enemy comes in the end to seem a very small thing, a by-product. There had been nothing like this in English polemics before.[2]

Those inclined to doubt such a sweeping statement can consult Hooker's predecessors themselves, if they have the patience to read for more than a few dozen pages. A common method of polemic in this period was to print, paragraph by paragraph, the text of your adversary, and then proceed to critique it line by line. Naturally, this meant that the texts in question grew enormously in volume with each installment in the debate. It also meant a sometimes maddening repetitiveness, as similar points of dispute were taken up in many different places, and it created an atmosphere in which neither side felt at liberty to concede a single point, so that the vast majority of the debate was consumed with trivialities. Hooker renounced this method completely, declaring instead his intention to structure the work systematically, "that every former part might give strength unto all that follow, and every later bring some light unto all before" (I.1.2). Although he will occasionally quote his adversaries (as well as some authorities on his side) directly, these quotes are relatively sparse, and firmly subordinated to the orderly progression of the whole. Hooker was well aware that this approach would seem baffling to many of his contemporaries, who would be impatient for him to get right down to the point and start

---

2. *English Literature in the Sixteenth Century*, 459.

arguing, but insists that any argument that starts *in medias res*, rather than at the foundations, will never be resolvable.

Let us then take some time to survey the carefully-constructed edifice of the *Laws*; since the rest of this book will be organized thematically according to topics of particular interest to the contemporary reader, this will be our only chance to see, albeit in very brief outline form, how Hooker himself lays out his argument.

THE CHALLENGES TO BE ANSWERED

Before beginning, though, let us take a moment to get clear on just what the question at hand was, at least as Hooker understood it. We have mentioned already a series of Puritan and presbyterian challenges to the established church from the 1560s to the 1590s; what was the common concern that drove these?

The answer would certainly depend on exactly whom you asked, with very different emphases coming to the fore at different times. The root concern, however, was *edification*.[3] The dissenters in the Vestiarian controversy of the 1560s were not just being stubbornly nitpicky. They knew that the Reformation in England was an exceedingly fragile thing, having nearly been extinguished by the five-year reign of Mary, and in danger of withering again should the political climate again become unfavorable. If it was to take deep root, the mass of the people must be truly converted and trained in the new faith. And given that these masses were liable to be influenced as much by visual symbolism as by explicit teaching, a truly reformed church must work to root out the visual markers of continuity with the Roman

---

3. So observed John S. Coolidge in a study that is by turns illuminating and frustratingly misleading, *The Pauline Renaissance in England*.

church, which might continue to lead the ignorant astray. If the priest still wore more or less the same garments, and followed much the same order of service, and still used the sign of the cross, etc., many churchgoers would assume that not much of great significance had changed. This was all the more so given that good Protestant preaching was hard to come by; most ministers were uneducated, and often had to serve multiple parishes, overseen by bishops with overwhelming administrative responsibilities. It took the better part of four decades to rectify these problems, and many of the more zealous ministers felt that the authorities were not prioritizing educated preaching (and in point of fact, Queen Elizabeth herself said as much, being suspicious of too much preaching).

For many Puritans, as they came to be called, this was more or less as far as it went: liturgical reform to root out superstition, administrative reform to ensure godly church discipline, and the reform of preaching and teaching to fill the land with better knowledge of the gospel. For many, this entailed no revolutionary overhaul, even of the Book of Common Prayer, which they simply wanted liberty to use with flexibility, omitting un-edifying ceremonies. If the queen had been happy to grant that, it is possible that things would have gone no further.

But in a tense and conflict-ridden environment, it was natural that many should seek a higher standard to defend their claim to Christian liberty: Scripture. If Scripture tells us all that is needful for the upbuilding of the church, and pure liturgy is needful for the upbuilding of the church, then it would seem Scripture must tell us the details of worship and church order. And if it does, then to add to or change such details is to substitute man's word for God's, indeed, to engage in a species of idolatry. For such dissenters, then, it was no longer a matter of merely requesting the freedom for the minister to omit unedifying ceremonies as he sees fit, but insisting on his *obligation* to resist any unbiblical ceremonies. Logically, this move involved something of an inversion of the original claim to Christian liberty, and threatened to impose instead a new legalistic burden: instead of "nothing but what is in Scripture may be *required for belief*" it was now "nothing but what is in Scripture may be *used* or *believed*." The difference may be clear enough in retrospect, but in this polemically-charged environment, where whoever could pound on the Bible the hardest had the upper hand, the transition was easy to make. Thus arose the more radical brand of Puritanism, which I have called in my writing "precisianism," adopting another term used at the time by its critics.[4] These "precisians," in their quest for what was most edifying, sought to find precise guidance in the Word of God for every area of life, but especially for ecclesiastical matters, and worried that failure to follow this guidance precisely was to invite God's judgment. Among the most radical, this entailed the conclusion that faithful Christians must separate entirely from the national church and worship in their own conventicles, so as to avoid the wrath to come.

Frequently associated with such precisianism, though logically distinct from it, was the presbyterian movement. As we have seen in the previous chapter, presbyterian convictions were quick to emerge in a context where the bishops seemed to be hindering the progress of the gospel and of pure worship. Those who were looking to Scripture for guidance on all that was edifying, and finding that the bishops were clearly *not* edifying, were not surprised to find in Scripture a platform of church government opposed to bishops. The details were hazy at first, but gradually (over

---

4. See chapter 3 of my dissertation, *Freedom of a Christian Commonwealth*, forthcoming from Eerdmans, 2016.

a period of roughly a century, in fact) the system we now know as presbyterianism coalesced, built upon two main premises: (1) there must be no standing inequality among ordained ministers (i.e., no bishops with spiritual authority over other ministers); (2) to assist them in the government of individual churches, and especially in the important business of church discipline, each minister must have a team of "lay-elders" (though these were often treated as another rank of quasi-clergy) drawn from the membership.

Although rarely explicitly stated by either precisians or presbyterians, one other all-important challenge was raised by their proposed reforms: the challenge to the royal supremacy. In England, as in the vast majority of territories that accepted the Protestant Reformation, the reformation was to some extent engineered, and at the very least advanced and protected, by civil authorities. The exact extent of civil authority over church affairs differed from polity to polity, but the general principle was accepted by all the leading Reformers; after all, was it not their contention that *all* believers, laity as well as clergy, had access to God's word and could have authority in the church? If so, then why not the ruler, the *praecipuum membrum ecclesiae*, or "foremost member of the church"?[5] However, by insisting that the church must be comprehensively reformed in all its details according to the law of Scripture, as interpreted by Puritan ministers, the precisianist platform implied that the queen, while retaining supremacy in name, would in fact lose any discretionary authority over the Church, following instead the dictates of her clergy at every point. This sounded to many of her supporters like a new papalism.

---

5. This terminology comes from Melanchthon, though the concept was widely shared, especially among Lutherans. See Avis, *Church in the Theology of the Reformers*, ch. 9, for a good discussion of this theme.

The presbyterian platform was even worse; by decentralizing church government, and making the lay-elders in each church the only legitimate bearers of authority among the laymen, the presbyterians would appear to render the queen's office almost entirely obsolete when it came to religious affairs, whatever their protests to the contrary. This sounded like a form of Anabaptism.[6]

These, then, are the three great challenges that Hooker's *Laws* is constructed to meet: (1) a strict biblicism, (2) presbyterian church order as the necessary biblical form of church government, and (3) the challenge to the unity of the civil and ecclesiastical orders and the authority of the queen in particular. Of these, Hooker recognized, the first was the key, the spring from which the other problems flowed. However, it should be noted that the *Laws* was not merely a refutation. Again breaking rank from many of his predecessors, Hooker also tried to address head-on the concern about edification, which had started the whole debate and was for many Puritans still the chief issue. Large sections of the *Laws* are therefore dedicated to showing not merely that the structure and worship of the English church is *legitimate*, but that it is actively edifying to the spiritual health of the people and the whole commonwealth.

It is important to add, moreover, that we would be wrong to read the *Laws*, as many have done, as an unapologetic defense of the status quo, whatever that status quo might be—as Diarmaid MacCulloch memorably put it, "If the parliamentary legislation of 1559 had laid down that English clergy were to preach standing on their heads, then Hooker would have found a theological reason for justifying it."[7] The fact is, however, that far from being a paid shill of

---

6. For an acute analysis, see O'Donovan, *Theology of Law and Authority*, ch. 8.

7. *Reformation*, 507.

the powers that be, Hooker appears to have written primarily for his own satisfaction,[8] and like most writers of good theology, made hardly any money off the publication. This gave him the freedom to subtly critique existing arrangements even when he appeared to be defending them, as Hooker scholar Daniel Eppley has recently argued.[9] Indeed, such subtle dissent may account for the fact that it took five decades for Books VI–VIII of the *Laws* to see the light of day.

A BRIEF TOUR OF THE *LAWS*

Before getting into the meat of his argument, Hooker opens his work with an extended Preface addressed "to them that seek (as they term it) the reformation of Laws, and orders Ecclesiastical, in the Church of England." Here he makes a direct appeal (how genuine, scholars have debated) to the hearts and minds of his opponents, exhorting them to see the dangerous and unstable course they have set out upon. Although frequently glossed over, especially in older works, the Preface is one of the most fascinating, perceptive, and still-relevant portions of the *Laws*. In it, Hooker displays an understanding of mass psychology and apocalypticism that is remarkably ahead of his time, anticipating many of the insights of contemporary sociologists and political theorists.[10] He begins with an account of Calvin's church order at Geneva, praising it for its wisdom, but deploring how Calvin himself, and even more so his followers, claimed

---

8. As MacCulloch himself notes elsewhere ("Richard Hooker's Reputation," 572). See further Patrick Collinson, "Richard Hooker and the Elizabethan Establishment," 165–71.

9. Eppley, "Practicing What He Preaches."

10. Indeed, the renowned political theorist Eric Voegelin was to draw attention to these insights in his *New Science of Politics*, 135–42.

direct divine sanction for it. (Hooker is later in the *Laws* consistent enough to refuse to claim such sanction even for his cherished episcopacy, though he thinks that it has much more divine warrant than others.)

In considering why Calvin's system should have been proposed in England, Hooker makes the perceptive observation that people are quick "to impute all faults and corruptions, wherewith the world aboundeth, unto the kind of ecclesiastical government established" (Pref. 3.8), which we might well generalize to include government in general. Having become convinced that the established order is the source of all their problems, Hooker notes that the people are easily swayed to adopt whatever makes the strongest claim for divine authority, and once they get it into their heads that Scripture teaches something, it is easy to dismiss any naysayers as lukewarm time-servers. Rather, "the absolute commandment of almighty God must be received although the world by receiving it should be clean turned upside down" (Pref. 8.5). It is this, says Hooker, which constitutes the greatest danger of the presbyterian movement; presbyterianism in itself would represent a pretty dramatic and disruptive overhaul of the English polity, but much more serious is the basic psychological and hermeneutical error. Once the principle is adopted that all authority but the private authority of the Word of God is automatically suspect, there is no telling where a new religious movement will end up, as he shows by referencing the excesses of some Anabaptists and other sixteenth-century sects.

Of course, he does not wish, he says, to simply squelch well-meant conscientious objections; he takes the Protestant doctrine of Christian liberty too seriously for that. But he does make an earnest appeal for the dissenters to examine their consciences to see whether their judgments are so sure as they think, and if there is any uncertainty in them, to recognize their duty to suspend their judgment in obedience to authority for the sake of common peace and order.

Order is indeed one of Hooker's great preoccupations in the *Laws*, and receives its most luminous and compelling portrayal in Book I. Entitled "Concerning Laws, and their several kinds in general," this book aims to lay a foundation for Hooker's entire argument by considering carefully the relation of natural laws, divine laws, and human laws. His precisianist opponents, he thinks, have oversimplistically opposed divine laws and human laws as the only two types—there are either the laws which God commands in Scripture, or the laws which human authorities command. Sure, they concede, there may be some relatively insignificant areas where human authorities are left discretion to make their own laws (though Hooker will find some statements from Cartwright which cast doubt even on this concession), but in all areas of importance, God has given us laws, and obviously these divine laws are to be preferred above human laws. But this, argues Hooker, is to fundamentally misunderstand the logic of both human laws and divine laws, treating them almost as mere arbitrary commands grounded in the authority of the lawmaker. On the contrary, both are grounded in *wisdom*, wisdom which considers the good of those governed, and how to achieve that good in particular circumstances. And this is ultimately grounded in the *eternal law*, the order of the divine wisdom by which God regulates his own actions, and governs the world he has created. Because God created a rational world, the order of divine wisdom is reflected in the order of creation, which thus participates in a creaturely fashion in the eternal law.

This participation takes three forms, corresponding to three orders of creature: the law of nature (governing the natural order), the celestial law (governing angels), and the law of reason (governing human beings who apprehend the natural order rationally). From this latter arises human law, a specification and binding imposition of the law of reason to enable us to live together in political society. And because of the fall, all these laws must be supplemented with divine law, which restates more clearly the teachings of reason and supplements them with the revelation of the way of salvation in Jesus Christ. But while going beyond earthly laws, divine law in no way contradicts or overturns them, since in redemption God reaffirms and perfects his creation, rather than destroying or ignoring it. Accordingly, we ought not presuppose a tension between biblical commands and our moral intuitions or civil laws; to be sure, we are fallen and so will frequently encounter such tensions, but they are not inevitable—the opposition between God and the devil does not entail a necessary opposition between Christ and the world.

With this foundation in mind, we may move much more quickly through the following books of the *Laws*. The title of Book II gives us a pretty good idea of its contents: "Concerning their first position who urge reformation in the Church of England: Namely, that Scripture is the only rule of all things which in this life may be done by men." Clearly, as Hooker has described the position, it is something of a *reductio ad absurdum*: who could really claim that Scripture contains the rule, except in the most general terms, for every kind of human action in any context? And yet Hooker does not have difficulty finding precisians that speak this way (notably Cartwright), nor would we find difficulty finding conservative Christians of various stripes today who use similar language. To expose the contradictions inherent in this position, Hooker will elaborate on his remarks concerning the law of reason in Book I, insisting that we honor the manifold forms in which divine Wisdom is mediated to humankind:

> As her ways are of sundry kinds, so her manner of teaching is not merely one and the same. Some things she openeth by the sacred books of Scripture; some things by the glorious works of Nature: with some things she inspireth them from above by spiritual influence; in some things she leadeth and traineth them only by worldly experience and practice. We may not so in any one special kind admire her, that we disgrace her in any other; but let all her ways be according unto their place and degree adored. (II.1.4)

Some of Hooker's most perceptive and enduring insights are to be found in this book, in particular his realization of how thoroughly the precisianists, while beginning by defending the freedom of the Christian conscience, have ended by thoroughly undermining it. If we demand scriptural warrant for everything, asks Hooker, "what shall the Scripture be but a snare and a torment to weak consciences, filling them with infinite perplexities, scrupulosities, doubts insoluble, and extreme despairs?" (II.8.6).

This sets the stage for a more specific application of this question, in relation to the issue of church polity, in Book III. Again, the title is clear enough: "Concerning their second assertion, that in Scripture there must be of necessity contained a form of Church-polity, the laws whereof may in nowise be altered." Here Hooker has occasion to elaborate on his discussion of the relation of human and divine laws from Book I. There are laws that are divine in the sense that they are contained in Scripture, but that are within the sphere of human law inasmuch as they prescribe changeable policies for particular political and social structures. This is true of the church as much as the state, since as a visible organized institution, the church partakes of the same earthly character as other human societies. We will have much more to say about this book in chapter 10

("Church"), but suffice to say that Hooker here seeks to demonstrate that the details of church polity are simply not the sort of thing that we should *expect* Scripture to address comprehensively and unchangeably. We cannot therefore, as some of the presbyterians had, simply insist up front that Scripture must contain such information, and interrogate it until it yields the desired conclusion; we must let Scripture itself determine the scope of its own perfection.

With the key precisianist and presbyterian challenges thus parried, Hooker moves to address the Puritan concern which started the whole controversy: that the Church of England's rites were unedifying and too prone to popish superstition. Book IV will address these charges in a general form before he turns to address specific objections in Book V. In countering the general charges, Hooker is able to lay out his approach to the authority of church tradition. On the one hand, the church is an institution in history, and as history changes, the church may in certain ways change along with it, so that she does not need to feel bound to do everything just as it was done in the first century, or to justify every current practice by patristic authority. At the same time, history does have weight and ought not be ignored, and if once a practice has taken root, it should not be lightly scorned, but carefully weighed. On these bases, Hooker is able to justify the substantial continuities with medieval liturgy and structure that remained in the Church of England after the Reformation; just because popery is wicked does not mean that a pure church must purge itself of any point of resemblance with the Roman church.

We might expect Book V, the huge and sprawling series of responses to all the particular Puritan scruples concerning the Book of Common Prayer, to be the most tedious portion of the *Laws*, of historical interest only. But in fact it is one of the liveliest and most-quoted sections, for at least three reasons. First, many of these liturgical debates—whether over the observance of the church calendar, the role of music in liturgy, the use of set prayers, the administration of the sacraments, etc.—remain as alive as ever, particularly within more conservative churches. Presbyterians today will raise just the same objections they did more than four hundred years ago, and Anglicans can continue to respond by turning to Hooker. Second, Hooker is always careful, even here, to stick to his method of turning first to general principles before adjudicating the particular question at hand. So we are treated in the course of Book V to fascinating reflections on the role of liturgy in general, the way in which temporal rhythms structure our lives, why God desires us to pray, and the efficacy of the sacraments. Third, this last discussion, on the sacraments, is preceded by the closest thing to a bit of systematic theology in the *Laws*: a seven-chapter exposition of the doctrine of the incarnation, and our union with Christ, that remains a landmark of Reformed Christology. A number of scholars have noted that this discussion stands at the structural heart of the *Laws*, anchoring the whole text in a way that makes it quite literally Christocentric.

Books VI through VIII, where Hooker turns to answer the particular planks of the presbyterian platform of church government, were never published in his lifetime, and when they did come out several decades later, they were clearly incomplete. Of these, Book VI is the most fragmentary, to the point where scholars have argued over whether what we have is even any part of what Hooker intended as Book VI. The announced intention of Book VI is to address the presbyterian insistence on the necessity of lay-elders in the church, but the relatively short discussion we have is occupied entirely with a treatment of confession and penance. It would appear that, considering the chief task of lay-elders to be church-discipline, and the chief end of church discipline to be penance, Hooker intended this discussion as an introductory foundation to the question at hand. The evidence of Hooker's correspondence suggests that he had completed a rough draft at least of the rest of the argument, but was in the midst of revising it substantially at his death, and none of it survives.

Book VII comprises Hooker's defense of episcopacy in general, and in the particular form in which it existed in Elizabeth's church. The first, it must be said, is more persuasive than the second. Hooker makes a compelling biblical and historical case for episcopacy, while stopping short of insisting upon it as a matter of unchangeable necessity. But many Puritans, while not objecting to bishops in the abstract, nevertheless objected to the fact that those in Elizabeth's church were less pastors than courtiers and administrators, and, it often appeared, greedy and ambitious courtiers at that (though recent research has suggested this perception was largely unfair).[11] While Hooker could reasonably plead that the existing state of ecclesiastical administration was perhaps the best that could be managed at present, he sometimes went further than this and sought to provide a positive case for why bishops could and even should be wealthy noblemen, which most modern readers will find to be among the weaker sections of the *Laws*. However, Hooker ends the book with a scathing critique of some of the corruptions among the Elizabethan episcopate, thus partially redeeming himself for his apparent acceptance of the status quo.

Most readers come into Book VIII with a similar skepticism. Trained by the last couple of centuries to be profoundly skeptical of the entanglement of religion and

---

11. See for instance Collinson, *Religion of Protestants*, ch. 2; Fincham, *Prelate as Pastor*, ch. 4.

politics, and taught by generations of religious dissenters to lament the "Erastian" subjection of the church to the state, we expect to find Hooker's *apologia* for the royal supremacy in the church, the focus of this chapter, to be profoundly outdated and downright distasteful. And to be sure, it is anachronistic, but the extraordinary thing is that, by the logic of Book VIII itself, Hooker himself might have been the first to admit that. That is to say, unlike almost all prior defenses of the royal supremacy, Hooker does not turn to the example of the godly kings of ancient Israel to insist that God has simply ordained that the civil magistrate have supreme authority over religious administration. Rather, following the logic he has established in earlier books, he justifies it on grounds of natural law, human law, and history, insisting that it is a timeless principle of sound reason that all good commonwealths should be concerned with maintaining right religion, but that the form this takes is a matter of historical prudence.[12] Moreover, it is clear that his own preferred form is substantially more guarded and constitutional than that which in fact prevailed in Elizabethan England: he would like to see the monarch's authority as little more than a matter of final veto power, with most church policies actually being determined by the discretion of the bishops and learned men of the church, as eventually came to be the case in the development of the English constitution.

HOOKER'S STYLE

Hopefully this quick guided tour will give some sense already of why Hooker's work has continued to win so many

---

12. For a fuller discussion, see my article, "More than a Swineherd."

admirers through the centuries.[13] But any discussion of the *Laws* would be incomplete without reference to its famous prose style. We have quoted C. S. Lewis already that "the style is, for its purpose, perhaps the most perfect in English."[14] Yet its first readers were not very pleased. The author of *A Christian Letter* complained that these "books be so long and tedious, in a style not usual, and (as we verily think) the like hard to be found; far differing from the simplicity of holy Scripture, and nothing after the frame of the writings of the Reverend and learned Fathers of our church"[15] and repeatedly demanded that Hooker speak "plainly." Somewhat more impartially, but still not exactly flatteringly, Thomas Fuller famously summarized Hooker's style as "long and pithy, driving a whole flock of several clauses before he came to the close of a sentence."[16] And indeed, Hooker's ability to keep layering on dependent and independent clauses, one after another, before finally getting to the end of his sentence, has few parallels in the history of the language. There are even times where we feel Hooker must have been quite aware of his idiosyncrasy and just seeing how long he could drag out a sentence for fun.[17] But for the most part, this feature of Hooker's writing—a common feature of eloquent Latin syntax, it should be noted, but only rarely attempted in English—appears to be neither a quirk or a flaw, but a conscious device. Lewis explains:

---

13. For a much more extensive outline of the argument of the *Laws*, see the excellent "Tour of the Laws" in McGrade's introduction to the new Oxford edition of the work, I: xxxi–xciv.

14. *English Literature in the Sixteenth Century*, 462.

15. *Christian Letter*, FLE 4:71.

16. Fuller, *Church History of Britain*, III:128.

17. See for instance the 528-word sentence in V.76.8.

> The Latin syntax is there for use, not ornament; it enables him, as English syntax would not, to keep many ideas, as it were, in the air, limiting, enriching, and guiding one another, but not fully affirmed or denied until at last, with the weight of all that thought behind him, he slowly descends to the matured conclusion. The structure mirrors the real movement of his mind.[18]

Not merely the movement of his mind, but, we might add, of the *Laws* as whole. Just as he insists on making sure we grasp all the relevant principles at stake before he comes to offer particular conclusions on any disputed matter, so on the level of each sentence, he does not hastily state his mind until has added all the relevant considerations and qualifications. In an extraordinarily illuminating essay on Hooker's style, Georges Edelen summarizes,

> The syntactical order reflects the temporal and logical priority given to premise, evidence, condition, and cause over conclusion. By first exploring the reasons for his position, even to the extent of admitting a subjective bias, Hooker suggest that his conclusion comes only as the result of a rational process of investigation; by treating each element in the argument with syntactic discursiveness, he implies that he has scrupulously examined each link in the chain; by casting the entire chain as a single sentence, he emphasizes the logical coherence of his thought. The structure of Hooker's sentences has much to do with his reputation for judiciousness.[19]

For this reason, although Hooker is certainly capable of glorious and almost lyrical passages (as, for instance, at

---

18. *English Literature in the Sixteenth Century*, 462.
19. "Hooker's Style," 248–49.

the end of the discussion of the Eucharist, or the beginning of that on church music), Hooker's style is mostly something of an acquired taste, requiring a disciplined and patient reader, but offering a unique satisfaction. This is particularly so of Hooker's humor, which, as we have come to expect of British humor in general, thrives on understatement and irony. His putdowns, coming as they do often at the end of long suspended sentences, can be easily missed, but delightfully devastating when noticed.

Clearly, though, these putdowns are not mere idle jabs for amusement, but reflect a carefully-conceived agenda. What is this agenda? How, in other words, does Hooker understand himself in relation to the Puritans he is responding to, and what exactly does he hope to accomplish with this great literary undertaking? To answer these questions, let us turn to consider Hooker's vision and aims.

FOR DISCUSSION

1. Why does C. S. Lewis describe Hooker's work as "a revolution in the art of controversy"?
2. In what ways could Elizabeth's churchmen see Puritan/presbyterian convictions as a challenge to key Protestant principles?
3. How is the ground-laying in Bk. I of the *Laws* important to Hooker's larger task?
4. How does Hooker's literary style support his argumentative method?

4

HOOKER AS PROTESTANT

A CATHOLIC SYMPATHIZER?

It may seem odd to dedicate a chapter to the proposition that Richard Hooker was a Protestant—what else would he be?—but Hooker's Protestant orthodoxy has been questioned since at least 1599, when the authors of *A Christian Letter* wrote, "It seemed unto us that covertly and underhand you did bend all your skill and force against the present state of our English church: and by color of defending the discipline and government thereof, to make questionable and bring in contempt the doctrine and faith itself."[1] Since that time, there have been Catholic sympathizers and even converts (such as King James II) who claimed Hooker's support, and from the nineteenth century on, Anglo-Catholics who sought to make Hooker a foundation-stone of their halfway house between Protestantism and Rome.

This was the easier to do, as Hooker clearly stood apart from many of his contemporaries in his relatively charitable attitude toward the church of Rome. You will recall that it was this attitude—"I doubt not but God was merciful to save

1. *FLE* 4:7.

thousands of our fathers living in popish superstitions, inasmuch as they sinned ignorantly"[2]—which earned Walter Travers's ire at the Temple and plunged Hooker into public controversy. Of course, this concession does not seem to us today to be a very great one—Hooker still contends firmly that those who knowingly defended the Catholic doctrine of justification were damnable—and later ecumenists have read too much into Hooker's statements just as Travers did.[3] To be sure, many have also pointed to Hooker's insistence at various points in the *Laws* (to the disgruntlement of the authors of *A Christian Letter*) that the church of Rome was indeed still part of the visible church of Christ, as further evidence of his *rapprochement* with Rome. However, this contention was less the effect of an attempt to rehabilitate Rome than it was of Hooker's very minimalistic definition of what it meant to be part of the visible church. Moreover, as Paul Avis has shown,[4] there had long been differing interpretations among leading Protestant theologians of the exact status of the church of Rome, with the English Puritans being unusual, rather than representative, in their wholesale condemnation of it. Nonetheless, the later concerted attempt of some "Laudian" churchmen in the 1620s–40s to downplay differences with Rome has led a great many interpreters of Hooker to mistakenly read him through the lens of this later discussion. None of this is to deny, mind you, that Hooker may be appropriated as a valuable ecumenical resource, but we must beware of anachronism.

---

2. Hooker, *Answer to the Supplication*, in *FLE* 5:249.

3. See Bauckham, "Hooker, Travers, and the Church of Rome," for an excellent analysis of how this controversy has been widely misunderstood, with Hooker substantially in line with other leading Protestant apologists of his day in his assessment of the Church of Rome.

4. Avis, "The True Church in Reformation Theology"; also, *Church in the Theology of the Reformers*, ch. 3.

So we would be fair to assume, I think, that Hooker is a robustly Protestant theologian, seeing himself as walking in the footsteps of Luther, Calvin, Peter Martyr Vermigli, and the great early apologist of the Church of England, John Jewel, whom Hooker calls "the worthiest divine that Christendom hath bred for the space of some hundreds of years" (II.6.4). There is much in his writings to attest this self-understanding, and nothing, on closer consideration, that calls it into question. But the question remains, "what sort of Protestant?" He is not, I think we can safely say, an especially Lutheran theologian, though it is worth pointing out that we should not discount any Lutheran influences. Even on the Continent, where the conflict between Reformed and Lutheran had been sharp, many Reformed theologians of the 1580s and 1590s did not see their rift as a *fait accompli*, and theologians such as Zacharius Ursinus and Girolamo Zanchi had done their best to bridge the gap. In England, early Lutheran influence in the Reformation of the 1530s had been largely supplanted by Reformed influence in the 1550s and 1560s, though moderate Lutherans like Melanchthon and mediating figures like Martin Bucer clearly exercised a considerable influence on several churchmen and perhaps more importantly, on the queen herself. Hooker's contemporary Lancelot Andrewes, who was to have so much influence on the Jacobean church, appears to have read deeply in the Lutheran theologians.[5] It would not be surprising if Hooker had done so as well, thus accounting for some of his less Calvinistic emphases. Of course, contemporary Reformation scholarship has increasingly recognized that "Calvinistic" and "Reformed" ought not to be taken as necessarily synonymous, with theologians like Heinrich Bullinger and Peter Martyr Vermigli, along with a

---

5. See McCullough, ed., *Lancelot Andrewes: Selected Sermons and Lectures*, xx.

host of other thinkers, leaving just as deep a stamp on many developing Reformed churches in the sixteenth century. So there were in fact a fairly wide range of "Reformed-ish" options on the theological spectrum of the 1580s and 1590s that Hooker might have occupied, a fact that has until now not been readily appreciated in Hooker studies.

A REFORMED THEOLOGIAN?

More recently, then, the discussion has become considerably more nuanced, focusing chiefly on the question of whether Hooker's theology challenged, either implicitly or explicitly, the understood consensus of English Reformed theology of his day. Can we really call Hooker "Reformed," or should we call him "Anglican" or something else entirely? Now at this point, many readers might ask a very fair question: why does it matter? Why, that is, should we expend much time and energy in figuring out exactly what label to slap on Hooker, if he defies easy labels? Why not simply expound Hooker's thought on its own terms?

A few points might be made in answer, but perhaps the most important is to say that no one's thought can be expounded simply *on its own terms*. Every thinker has a context, and based on that context, presupposes any number of things in his audience, which he may not state expressly in his writing. Without knowing these unwritten assumptions, we cannot always know just what is being said and what isn't. Moreover, no writer can be close to exhaustive, and necessarily leaves us many gaps to fill in. This is true of Hooker particularly, who never wrote anything like a systematic theology. One of the ways the interpreter fills in such gaps, just like a paleontologist reconstructing incomplete dinosaur skeletons, is by asking, "What did similar contemporary thinkers say on these points?" But that, of course, requires us to determine who are the most similar, and thus most relevant, points of comparison. In the present case, given his clearly Reformed context, we should start from the assumption that he reasons from a roughly Reformed standpoint, and only revise this in the face of contrary evidence. But is there such contrary evidence?

This, after all, was the chief charge of *A Christian Letter*: that Hooker was opposing the theological standards of the Thirty-Nine Articles, as they had been interpreted by leading English Protestants since 1560. With the work of Peter Lake and his disciples, the testimony of the *Christian Letter* has been taken quite seriously as "a telling indication of how Hooker's remarks were received and interpreted by his principal target audience,"[6] suggesting that we should see Hooker as advancing a different kind of Protestantism, at least, from the standard Reformed orthodoxy of his day. Indeed, Lake is convinced that the moderate Puritan standpoint of the *Christian Letter*, with its high Calvinism and virulent anti-Romanism, must be taken as representing not merely the theological center of gravity in Elizabeth's church, but its quasi-authoritative consensus.[7] In relation to this consensus, he has argued, Hooker clearly presages many of the developments that were to be called English Arminianism a couple decades later and which, after the English Civil War, were to become woven into the theology of the Church of England to create a distinctive "Anglican" branch of Protestantism.

Torrance Kirby, on the other hand, has firmly rejected the testimony of the *Christian Letter* as little better than a run-of-the-mill polemical slander, such as one regularly encounters in theological disputation; after all, the letter seeks to impugn not merely Hooker's Reformed or Protestant credentials, but even his very Trinitarian orthodoxy,

---

6. Joyce, *Anglican Moral Theology*, 60.
7. See for instance his article, "Business as Usual?"

charges which no serious scholar takes seriously. Against such testimony, says Kirby, we must set Hooker's own clear self-representation in the *Laws*, "Think not that ye read the words of one who bendeth himself as an adversary against the truth which ye have already embraced; but the words of one who desireth even to embrace together with you the self-same truth, if it be the truth" (Pref. 2.3). This and other such statements clearly suggest that Hooker intends his theology to be taken not merely as continuous with the magisterial Reformers, but as essentially consonant with the standards of Reformed orthodoxy in his day (even if he thinks some English Protestants have fallen out of touch with them). The sincerity of his intent, thinks Kirby and many interpreters of his school, is clearly borne out by a careful analysis of key theological claims within his work.

The persistence of questions concerning Hooker's Protestant or at the very least Reformed credentials stems from at least five factors. First, it is important to recognize that despite the length of the *Laws*, we really do not have a huge volume of theological writing from Hooker: much of the *Laws* itself is concerned with concrete questions of liturgy and polity, and his other writings are slim. It seems likely that, as with most theologians, his thought developed with age and experience (his earliest extant work dates from age twenty-eight or twenty-nine, the latest from age forty-six), but we simply don't have enough to go on to trace this development clearly, especially as the latest works are fragmentary and unfinished. The second factor, it must be said, is the elusiveness of Hooker's thought; he does not state himself as forthrightly as he might on certain key points, partly to avoid digressing from his apologetic agenda, partly on account of his circumlocutory style, and partly, perhaps, to avoid needless controversy. However, this elusiveness has been overstated. On many points of consequence, his statements are quite precise and to the point, and have simply been missed by readers lacking in theological literacy or expecting him to say something different. The third factor is thus the long, vague tradition of Anglicanism, and the supposition on the part of many readers that since Hooker is an "Anglican" he must say what that tradition is supposed to say (even when he clearly doesn't). The fourth is the profound insularity of much scholarship on Hooker, which is simply unaware of the vast and enormously sophisticated theological literature of his Reformed contemporaries outside of England, or even of foundational Reformers such as Bullinger and Vermigli. To properly assess the status of Hooker's theology, it would seem, we must have recourse to the international standards of Reformed orthodoxy at this time, as defined by the theology being taught at such centers as Geneva, Zurich, Heidelberg, Leiden, and even Königsberg. This has in fact only just begun to be undertaken by the latest scholarship. The fifth point, however, is the originality, or at the very least the freedom, of Hooker's own thought. Although certainly not interested in novelty for novelty's sake, Hooker does seem to prefer to take up a problem and think it through afresh, in close dialogue with the history of Christian theology as well as the challenges of his own day, rather than simply echoing an established consensus. Sometimes this creates the illusion of difference where what we have is merely idiosyncratic expression; sometimes it reflects genuine theological originality.

Clearly this discussion is complex, and to even begin to adjudicate it would mire us in a dense thicket of primary and secondary literature, and force us to preempt discussion of some of the particular theological issues to be examined in chapters 8–11. But we can at least attempt here to summarize some of the chief points where Hooker's Protestant credentials have been debated, and take note of the current state of the debate on each of these points.

DISPUTED POINTS

Scripture and Reason

Perhaps one of the most obvious challenges to Hooker's Protestant commitment comes at the point that is indeed a chief focus of the *Laws*: his doctrine of Scripture. The Reformation, it is often noted, was built upon two chief pillars: the *material principle*—justification by faith alone—and the *formal principle*—the sole authority of Scripture. To question the authority of Scripture and erect another norm in its place—whether church authorities, or tradition, or human reason—was to depart from Protestantism at one of its most crucial points. Many later Anglicans were to take such departure as a point of pride, caricaturing the Reformed doctrine as a narrow individualistic biblicism and crediting Hooker with the invention of the "Anglican tripod" or "threefold cord": Scripture, reason, and tradition.[8] Hooker certainly never formulates the matter that way, and his understanding of both "reason" and "tradition" were quite different than what these terms later came to mean in eighteenth and nineteenth-century Anglicanism.[9] But did he, in any case, suggest that Scripture was not after all the sole authoritative standard for Christian faith and practice? There are really at least two distinct issues here: the *ground* of Scripture's authority, and the *scope* and *mode* of Scripture's authority.

On the first point, it had seemed important to many Protestants to say that, if Scripture was indeed the highest standard for Christian faith, our trust in Scripture must not

---

8. For a contemporary defense of this view, see Gibbs, "Hooker's *Via Media* Doctrine of Scripture and Tradition."

9. For a good survey, see Neelands, "Scripture, Reason, and Tradition."

be grounded on anything else outside of Scripture. Rather, as Calvin particularly insisted, to remain fully authoritative, Scripture must be "self-authenticating": we believe it only on the basis of its own testimony. But Hooker appears to deny just this idea quite clearly in *Laws* I.14.1 and III.8.13–15, affirming that both reason and the church have a role in leading us to believe Scripture. These passages, and their relation to Calvin's ideas, have been the subject of heated debate in recent decades, and the discussion remains unresolved, although a forthcoming essay by Andrew Fulford helpfully points out that there were, in any case, other Reformed views on this issue besides Calvin's, so the difference may not be that important after all.[10]

On the second point, some in Hooker's day and ours have imagined that to honor Scripture rightly, we must treat it as the sole authority in all areas of life. Hooker has no patience for this kind of biblicism, considering that it is fact a dishonor to God and his many modes of natural revelation, and that the attempt to apply it practically ends in absurdity. Some have seen Hooker's defense of natural reason's role in Christian ethics and politics to be an abridgement of the Protestant commitment to *sola Scriptura*, but in fact, as has in recent years become particularly clear, his theology on this point was substantially the same as that of all the leading Reformers. These all taught doctrines of natural law and of *adiaphora*, the "things indifferent," on which Scripture was largely silent and prudence and reason must be our guide.[11] Many still worry that Hooker displays more confidence than the Reformers in the power of human reason to

---

10. Fulford, "'A Truth Infallible.'"

11. On natural law, see for instance, among many other studies, Grabill, *Rediscovering the Natural Law*. On adiaphora, see Verkamp, *The Indifferent Mean*.

interpret and apply Scripture, even if few seem able to pin down exactly where the difference lies.[12]

In any case, Hooker clearly remains a valuable resource for Protestants who are uneasy with the kind of fideistic biblicism that prevails in many conservative churches; the extent to which his approach entails any discontinuity from the magisterial Reformers remains somewhat unclear. We will return to look at these issues in more depth in chapter 8.

Soteriology

If Hooker's theology could be impugned for undermining the *formal principle* of the Reformation, we should not be surprised to find questions raised also regarding the *material principle*, justification by faith. Here, the *Christian Letter* led the charge,[13] even if its complaints have in fact been reinterpreted as a *virtue* of Hooker's theology by Anglican thinkers who think that the Protestant doctrine of justification tends toward antinomianism. Hooker, however, clearly thought these objections wildly off-base; no section of the *Christian Letter* elicited such ferocious retorts in the marginal notes as this one (including the memorable "ignorant ass!"). Indeed, Hooker expressed some surprise that his critics seemed to understand the Protestant doctrines of justification and sanctification so poorly themselves, and would have expressed similar surprise at many of his later interpreters.

---

12. See for instance Joan O'Donovan, *Theology of Law and Authority*, ch. 9, for an articulation of this nagging sense that Hooker gives too large a role to reason in interpreting Scripture. Nigel Voak's discussion of the issue in ch. 3 of his *Richard Hooker and Reformed Theology*, remains the fullest to date, though it suffers from a lack of attention to the full scope of Hooker's Reformed contemporaries.

13. See sections 6 and 7 in particular.

In the past couple decades, a consensus has increasingly emerged that at least in his direct statements on these issues, Hooker's formulations are thoroughly in line with his Reformed predecessors and contemporaries.[14] But some have nevertheless wondered whether or not these commitments are jeopardized by his doctrines of predestination and the sacraments. The latter we will turn to in a moment, and in more depth in chapter 11; the former warrants some brief remarks here. After all, although predestination may seem a matter for arid and abstract speculation, it impinges directly on justification; if we are saved by our own free choices, then are we not justified by our own works, rather than by passively receiving the merits of Christ? Nigel Voak has accordingly mounted a very sophisticated argument in his *Richard Hooker and Reformed Theology* that attempts to show that shifts in Hooker's thought on grace and the human will, as he wrote the *Laws*, drove him to a new understanding of justification which essentially conflicted with the Reformed doctrine.[15] Although impressive, Voak's argument is by his own admission something of a speculative reconstruction based on perceived internal tensions in Hooker's thought. Ranall Ingalls has since countered with a reading of Hooker on sin, grace, and justification that tries to reconcile these tensions in a way that accepts Hooker's protestation of fidelity to the magisterial reformers.[16]

Other aspects of Hooker's theology of predestination, however, have caught the attention of historians intent on reading him in light of the Arminian controversy that was to flare up in the Netherlands a few years after his death, and later to engulf the English church as well. The old school of

14. See most recently Baschera, "Righteousness Imputed and Inherent."

15. See especially ch. 4.

16. Ingalls, "Sin and Grace."

interpretation that imagined Hooker as paradigmatic representative of an Anglican *via media* consensus on this issue, neither Calvinist nor Pelagian (and so, roughly, Arminian) has been discredited, at least to the point that we now realize that among Hooker's contemporaries, some form of Calvinism was the clear consensus. But others, including Peter Lake and more recently Nigel Voak, believe that Hooker here anticipated the later development of such an Anglican Arminianism, with his own idiosyncratic attempt to moderate the harsh doctrines of high Calvinist predestinarianism, particularly on the question of the atonement.[17] On the other hand, their readings betray an apparent ignorance of the full scope and nuance of Reformed views at this time, and indeed in the decrees of the Synod of Dort itself.

Indeed, in many respects at least, Hooker's ideas may best be seen not as the anticipation of Arminius's, but of the moderate form of Calvinism, known as "hypothetical universalism," that was offered by John Davenant and other English delegates at Dort. This view, while accepting the unconditionality of predestination unto life, did not grant that predestination unto death (reprobation) was unconditional in the same sense. The saved could not point to their works, but to the grace of God only as the cause of their salvation, but the damned could only point to their works—their sin and rejection of God—as the cause of their damnation. Of course, this meant that it was necessary to affirm that saving grace was genuinely offered, in some real sense, to all people—something that Scripture seems to clearly affirm in several places, but which some Calvinists felt the need to

---

17. See especially *Richard Hooker and Reformed Theology*, ch. 5; and again, for a counterpoint, Ingalls, "Sin and Grace." It should be noted that these questions are particularly difficult to resolve given that Hooker's only direct treatment of the issue is found in the tantalizingly incomplete "Dublin Fragments."

deny. Hooker, then, and many later English Reformed theologians, insisted that it was wrong to speak of a "limited redemption," in which Christ only died for some, even if in practice the benefits of the atonement did not take effect for all.[18] If Hooker was, in fact, of a similar view to later moderate Calvinists like John Davenant or James Ussher, then he falls well within the Reformed consensus—indeed, some would argue closer to the earliest Reformed[19]—although certainly not within the form (so-called "five-point Calvinism") that has since become dominant. However, it is clear that Hooker's concern to soften what he saw as some of the most pastorally dangerous formulations of Calvinism drew the ire of many Puritan contemporaries, and continues to invite the scrutiny and debate of his interpreters today.

Sacraments, Liturgy, and Ecclesiology

One constellation of issues on which Hooker has seemed to many to be most "Anglican" is his rich sacramentology and high ecclesiology. Of course, these adjectives, "rich" and "high," despite their frequent use, often serve less to convey a clear doctrinal position than to mask the absence of one. It is not at all obvious exactly what they might mean when applied to Hooker, or how they might differentiate him from a Reformed or generally Protestant commitment. Peter Lake, however, has made these issues a centerpiece of his attempt to define Hooker's "invention of Anglicanism." By downplaying the centrality of preaching and enhancing the role of sacraments, common prayer, and liturgy, thinks Lake, Hooker "tended to conflate the two levels of the church's

---

18. See Snoddy, *Soteriology of James Ussher*, ch. 2 (esp. 69–74), and more fully, Lynch, "Richard Hooker and the Development of English Hypothetical Universalism."

19. See for instance Muller, review of *English Hypothetical Universalism*, by Jonathan D. Moore.

existence,"[20] that is, the visible and invisible, which were so sharply distinguished by many Protestant theologians before him. I shall argue in chapter ten that despite the influence of Lake's argument, it has difficulty explaining Hooker's own very pointed statements in the opposite direction.

On the other hand, no one can deny that Hooker speaks in very exalted (and beautiful) terms of the sacraments as instruments of the Christian's mystical union with Christ, and articulates a strong doctrine of the believer's real participation in Christ as the source of her salvation. This is not, in fact, very far from the language of Calvin himself,[21] or that of many other card-carrying Reformed theologians, even if it did rub some of his Puritan readers, like the author of the *Christian Letter*, the wrong way. But Hooker, far from considering himself an innovator, seemed surprised rather that his adversaries were so out of touch with the history and diversity of Reformed thinking on the sacraments. "You speak of sacraments as if by the space of these thirty or forty years you had lived in some cave of the earth and never heard [what] in these points the Church doth either vary or agree concerning them."[22]

Even if Hooker's sacramental theology was not so unusual after all, Lake is quite right to draw attention to Hooker's new emphasis on the role of symbolism and ritual as a means by which the believer is built up in faith and reverence. Most of the magisterial reformers, while considering liturgy to be generally adiaphorous or indifferent, preferred to err on the side of minimalism to avoid too much similarity with Rome or the risk of superstition. The Puritans in England, and particularly their stricter "precisianist" wing, considered the threat of superstition to be so

20. *Anglicans and Puritans*, 180.
21. See for instance Billings, *Calvin, Participation, and the Gift*.
22. *FLE* 4:38.

great that they questioned whether such liturgical matters were adiaphora at all, or rather should be outlawed since they were not found in Scripture. Even churchmen such as Whitgift who defended the Book of Common Prayer said little in defense of the disputed rites other than they were lawful and were edifying inasmuch as obedience to established law was always edifying. Hooker went considerably further in articulating a positive defense of vestments, festival days, the sign of the cross, and much more, and in so doing laid a foundation for a distinctively Anglican style of Christian devotion. At the same time, Hooker never goes beyond arguing that these rights are appropriate and "convenient"[23]—not necessary—so this unarguable shift in emphasis may not represent the foundational theological difference Lake seeks to discover. We will return to look at these issues in more depth in chapter 11.

Sources of His Theology

A final bone of contention, for the authors of the *Christian Letter* and on down to the present day, concerns the sources of Hooker's theology. The anonymous critic complained of Hooker's dishonor of Calvin and his contrasting honor of Aristotle and the medieval scholastics. And he has a fair point. Even if the substance of Hooker's theology is Reformational, very few of his citations are. This has naturally led many readers to wonder whether he is not, after all, trying to get back behind the Reformation, as an unfortunate recent episode, to drink directly from the well of the ancients and medievals. Given Luther's famous contempt for Aristotle and Calvin's slurs against "the schoolmen," what more

---

23. For the importance of Hooker's concept of "convenience," see Kindred-Barnes, *Richard Hooker's Use of History*.

evidence do we need, some have asked, that Hooker was not really all that Protestant?

This is yet another point, however, where recent scholarship has quite exploded old stereotypes, even if the insular scholarship of the English Reformation has been slow to catch up. As more and more Reformation sources have come to our attention, especially from the more scholastic writers like Melanchthon, Vermigli, and Zanchi, it has become clear that if Luther and Calvin really did dislike Aristotle and Aquinas,[24] they were perhaps the exception, rather than the rule. Even Hooker's moderate Puritan teachers at Oxford seem to have taught him a respect for the ancients and scholastics. Of course, the question remains as to why Hooker should quote so little from the magisterial Reformers, if he really did esteem them. Perhaps he was simply tired of the name-dropping that had become so typical of the polemical literature of his day, and Hooker would rather confine himself to more time-tested sources. Or perhaps it is a misguided question altogether; after all, Franciscus Junius's almost exactly contemporary Reformed treatise on law included not a single citation from any of the Reformers![25]

In short, then, it appears very likely that Hooker understood himself, and should be understood, as following more or less within the footsteps of the leading Protestant Reformers. Not only that, but if we had to place him more precisely, he would appear on most questions to fall fairly unproblematically within the broad and varied Reformed theological family that was developing so fruitfully at this time. This does not make him an uninteresting figure, simply restating established orthodoxies in a predictable form. Far from it. Hooker always remained his own man, and

---

24. Which has itself been increasingly thrown into doubt. See for instance, Muller, *The Unaccommodated Calvin*, ch. 3.

25. Franciscus Junius, *The Mosaic Polity*.

demonstrates a strikingly independent theological mind on many of the points that vexed his contemporaries.[26] But his novelty perhaps lies more in the way he reshuffled the existing deck of theological cards he had been dealt, rather than in introducing new cards into the deck. That is to say, he takes up many of the tensions that we see within the Reformed tradition, on issues such as the role of reason, the efficacy of the sacraments and role of liturgy, and the nature of predestination, and seeks to offer a creative synthesis within the general bounds of the tradition, though sometimes outside its mainstream. It is also clear that he had no interest in defining himself narrowly within a party label, but hoped to claim as much of the Christian tradition as possible—Reformed, Lutheran, the best of medieval Catholicism, and the Church Fathers. In this, perhaps more than anything, it can fairly be said that he prefigured the spirit of Anglican theology.

FOR DISCUSSION

1. Why does it matter how we label Hooker on a theological spectrum?
2. Why has Hooker's theological identity proven so elusive?
3. Does Hooker's approach to Scripture set him at odds with the Protestant Reformers? Why or why not?
4. Does Hooker's approach to sacraments and liturgy set him at odds with the Protestant Reformers? Why or why not?

---

26. Cf. Paul Avis, *In Search of Authority*, 96: "He is eclectic, discriminating, and not an exponent of any one school of thought. We should let Hooker be his own man."

5

HOOKER AS POLEMICIST

So we have established that Hooker saw and presented himself as a faithful Protestant. He also presented himself and perhaps saw himself as a faithful exponent of the Reformed tradition, and his Puritan adversaries as wayward sons of that tradition. Does it follow, then, that in the *Laws* we have nothing more than a heartfelt "irenical appeal to the hearts and minds and minds of the disciplinarian-Puritan opponents of the Elizabethan Settlement,"[1] a call to these wayward brothers to come home and reconcile? Well, no. It is clear that whether or not he desires reconciliation, he also at least clearly desires refutation, both for the sake of the erring Puritans and for other Englishmen, not least those in Parliament, who might be influenced by them. Hooker obviously wrote in part to satisfy himself, and probably also for posterity, as he himself declares at the beginning of the Laws. But we have already seen in chapter 1 that it is unrealistic to picture him as floating serenely above the polemical fray, occupied with timeless philosophical speculations or just wishing that everyone could get along.

---

1. Kirby, *Richard Hooker's Doctrine of the Royal Supremacy*, 20.

A POLEMICAL MASTERPIECE

His Preface, for all its irenic protestations, has an air of urgency and seriousness. Matters of great import, for the safety of the English church and state and the integrity of her theological commitment, are at stake, and those who with "wonderful zeal and fervor . . . have withstood the received orders of this Church" (Pref. 1.2) must be answered. Accordingly, Hooker sets himself the task of answering their critiques, and undermining their whole platform, and goes about it in a devastatingly effective way.[2] He marshals for the task not merely his immense knowledge of theological literature—from the patristics, scholastics, and his own age—and his understanding of syllogistic reasoning, but perhaps above all his rhetorical mastery of his medium. It is this last aspect that has received particularly sustained attention in recent years, as the picture of Hooker as "dovish and without gall" has given way to the picture of Hooker as the formidable polemicist.[3]

Indeed, this polemical edge appears even in his protestations of charity. Within the Preface itself, we begin with Hooker's complaint, uttered in tones of longsuffering resignation, that

> at your hands beloved in our Lord and Saviour Jesus Christ (for in him the love which we bear unto all that would but seem to be born of him, it is not the sea of your gall and bitterness that

---

[2]. Cf. Paul Avis: "Hooker is a highly effective controversialist who knows how to manipulate his readers to gain his ends. That does not mean that he was not seeking a change of heart and mind, a genuine conversion of his opponents; only that he goes about it in a formidably effective way" (review of *A Companion to Richard Hooker*, 416).

[3]. Rudolph Almasy's many essays on this subject are among the most important contributions to this discussion. See for instance, "They Are and Are Not Elymas," and "Rhetoric and Apologetics."

shall ever drown) I have no great cause to look for other than the selfsame portion and lot, which your manner hath been hitherto to lay on them that concur not in opinion and sentence with you. (Pref. 1.1)

From there, he enters on a brilliantly-crafted account of the establishment of Calvin's church discipline at Geneva, which highlights the levity and disorderliness of the Genevans and Calvin's sometimes too-high estimate of his own authority, while paying Calvin cleverly backhanded compliments: "incomparably the wisest man that ever the French Church did enjoy, *since the hour it enjoyed him*" (Pref. 2.1, emphasis mine). The next sections of the Preface dissect, in terms wonderfully incisive and entertaining, but no doubt maddening to the Puritans, just why and how it is that the presbyterian platform, so novel and implausible in itself, has gained such a wide and attentive hearing:

> First in the hearing of the multitude, the faults especially of higher callings are ripped up with marvelous exceeding severity and sharpness of reproof; which being oftentimes done begetteth a great good opinion of integrity, zeal, and holiness, to such constant reprovers of sin, as by likelihood would never be so much offended at that which is evil, unless themselves were singularly good. (Pref. 3.6)

> And the nature, as of men that have sick bodies, so likewise of people in the crazedness of their minds possessed with dislike and discontentment at things present, is to imagine that any thing (the virtue of which they hear commended) would help them; but that most which they have least tried. (Pref. 3.8)

> Most sure it is, that when men's affections do frame their opinions, they are in defense of error more earnest a great deal, than (for the most part) sound believers in the maintenance of truth apprehended according to the nature of that evidence which Scripture yieldeth. (Pref. 3.10)

He then moderates his tone, accepting that, while misguided in their beliefs, his opponents are really convinced of them, and dare not act against conscience. This requires some of his most delicate argumentation and rhetoric, in which he attempts to explain as winsomely as possible why sometimes, for the sake of peace and order, we must suspend the judgment of our own conscience in deference to the sentence of earthly authorities:

> Neither wish we that men should do any thing which in their hearts they are persuaded they ought not to do.... Be it that there are some reasons inducing you to think hardly of our laws. Are those reasons demonstrative, are they necessary, or but mere probabilities only? ... Any one such [demonstrative] reason dischargeth, I grant, the conscience, and setteth it at full liberty. But if the skilfullest amongst you can shew that all the books ye have hitherto written be able to afford any one argument of this nature, let the instance be given. (Pref. 6.3, 6.5)

This done, the Preface takes a more alarming turn, as Hooker expounds upon "how just cause there is to fear the manifold dangerous events likely to ensue upon this intended reformation, if it did take place" (Pref. 8), using the examples of the Anabaptists in particular. Here again, he carefully balances an acknowledgment that his adversaries may be pious and well-intentioned, and no doubt have few of these fearful consequences in mind, with a firm conviction that their errors are nonetheless too dangerous to simply be tolerated.

The Preface stands out among the text of the *Laws* for its fine-tuned rhetorical crafting, but examples of Hooker's carefully-conceived polemic could be found throughout the text of the *Laws*, even Book I, where he is laying the general foundations of his argument. At every point, we find that it is the very judiciousness and charitable restraint of Hooker's prose, his refusal to simply unload a torrent of polemical abuse, that renders it so polemically effective, earning for his own arguments the credibility of good judgment, and discrediting his opponents as stubborn, oversimplistic, or heedless of the dangerous implications of their views.

These dangerous implications, it should be said, are not simply those which are, in Hooker's view, politically dangerous, threatening the security of the fragile English Protestant state. Rather, he also deems them at points dangerous to the consciences of those very English Christians for whom his precisianist opponents appear to be so solicitous (a theme we shall return to in chapter 7). For instance, he worries that the Puritan overemphasis on preaching will actually denigrate the objective power of the Word of God, whether publicly or privately read:

> We have very just cause to stand in some jealousy and fear, lest by thus overvaluing their sermons, they make the price and estimation of Scripture otherwise notified to fall . . . [they say that] the principal cause of *writing* the Gospel was, *that it might be preached* upon or interpreted by public ministers apt and authorized thereunto. Is it credible that a superstitious conceit (for it is no better) concerning sermons should in such sort both darken their eyes and yet sharpen their wits withal? (V.22.7)

It should be obvious then to any attentive reader of the *Laws* that Hooker is passionately and polemically engaged throughout the text. Even where he withdraws from direct argument in order to examine foundational issues systematically—such as the law of reason in Book I or Christology in Book V—Hooker rarely loses sight of the larger polemical purpose.

"SMEAR TACTICS"?

However, a number of recent scholars have gone considerably further in emphasizing the polemical character of the *Laws*. In an influential 1972 essay, Reformation historian Cargill Thompson claimed that Hooker resorted to "calculated misrepresentation" and "smear tactics" in his "work of propaganda."[4] More recently, A. J. Joyce has dedicated an entire chapter of her *Richard Hooker and Anglican Moral Theology* to unmasking Hooker's "judicious" reputation as the result of a "skilfully constructed literary persona." "Hooker's pen," she says, "was fully capable of the most waspish, acerbic, and irreverent assaults, not only upon his puritan opponents, but . . . [also] upon Calvin himself."[5] Indeed, notwithstanding his frequent protestations of respect for his opponents and their Genevan hero, Joyce concludes that, after a careful literary deconstruction of his prose, we can conclude "that his opinion of both Calvin and his followers is seldom more than contemptuous."[6]

Now, I do not want to simply assume, hagiographically, that he must be innocent of all such charges of nastiness. It is certainly possible that he did feel this way, and accordingly felt little compunction in dishonestly twisting

4. Thompson, "Philosopher of the 'Politic Society,'" 14, 15, 13.

5. Joyce, *Anglican Moral Theology*, 51.

6. Ibid., 63.

the words of his opponents and scornfully dismissing them. The difficulty is that it is hard to find textual and historical justification for many of these claims. One is left rather with the impression that we must simply presuppose, on the basis of the "hermeneutic of suspicion" that dominates the humanities today, that any passage must be interrograted until it yields a sufficiently hostile reading. Joyce's lengthy treatment is a case in point, and warrants some careful attention and indeed criticism here.

For instance, if at any point Hooker appears to be complimentary to his opponents, Joyce deems that this may simply be chalked up to skillful sarcasm and irony, and the opposite meaning read into the text:

> He is, as we shall now see, more than ready both to damn with faint praise, and on other occasions to exaggerate his opponents' positive qualities, purely to enable him then to undercut them with devastating effectiveness. Indeed, ironically, part of the effectiveness of his demolition of his opponents' case comes from his purporting to take their claims with profound seriousness: this is in itself a highly successful and persuasive literary device.[7]

Now, to be sure, Hooker is a master of the backhanded compliment, of irony, and of rhetorical exaggeration. But it is clear that this hermeneutical method, applied persistently, can dissolve every text into a series of contradicting subtexts, and thus render the quest for meaning meaningless. For instance, although we have already noted the probable backhandedness in Hooker's compliment that Calvin was "incomparably the wisest man that ever the French church did enjoy," Joyce goes considerably further, singling out Hooker's use of the word "*French*." She suggests that perhaps

7. Ibid., 58.

he intended to summon up traditional English prejudices against the French, or even to associate Calvinism with the chaos tearing France apart in the early 1590s.[8] A much more straightforward explanation—i.e., that Calvin was a Frenchman who spent almost his entire life ministering in a French-speaking church on the borders of France, and helped frame the French Confession of Faith—is not considered.

Sometimes, though, Joyce does not even attempt to illustrate such irony, but simply asserts that Hooker is guilty of slanderous misrepresentation. Consider, for instance the passage noted above on the Puritan view of preaching, where Hooker summarizes with obvious irritation their account of why only the Word preached is effectual to salvation. Joyce cites it as a prime example of Hooker's tendency to "parody their stance in a way that is not merely barbed, but quite outrageous."[9] However, a consultation of the footnotes that are supplied in most editions of the *Laws* suggests that, far from a "parody," the passage is a close paraphrase of a passage from Puritan spokesman Thomas Cartwright's *Second Reply*,[10] and thus, although perhaps "barbed," is in no way "outrageous." There are a number of other points where Joyce does not pause to consider whether or not Hooker is faithfully representing the views that he is critiquing. The mere fact that he is critiquing them sharply and sometimes sarcastically is taken as evidence enough of a "merciless," "outrageous," and "contemptuous" treatment of his opponents.

This conflation of criticism and slander suggests that Joyce is evaluating Hooker not so much against the standard of a sixteenth-century theological controversialist, or even of most theological controversy nowadays, as against the

8. Ibid., 54n40.
9. Ibid., 51.
10. Specifically, 375.

standards of painfully nonconfrontational politeness that govern a committee meeting in a modern English parish or college. In such a setting, the mere voicing of passionately-felt disagreement is enough to scandalize, but it ought not be in our reading of Elizabethan literature. It may reflect also Joyce's anachronistic importation of the standards of contemporary academic journals, where strong personal convictions are supposed to be set aside as irrelevant, in favor of a thoroughly dispassionate and objective inquiry:

> Despite claiming that his aim is purely to establish the truth through an impeccably even-handed and impartial exploration of the issues involved, Hooker knows full well what his eventual conclusion will be, even before embarking upon the discourse . . . in his view they [the Puritans] need only look rationally at the evidence that he is so carefully . . . laying before them, and they will then see why he is correct and they are mistaken.[11]

A considerable portion of her reassessment of Hooker thus consists in revealing that he is not in fact doing something he never claims to be doing—suspending a passionate commitment to the truth as he understands it in order to seek a cordial meeting of the minds with his Puritan opponents on mutually-agreeable terrain. On the contrary, Hooker is convinced that his opponents are in error, and dangerously so, and that both for their own sakes and the sake of the commonwealth as a whole, the nature of this error needs to be exposed, as unbiblical, irrational, and seditious.

POLEMICAL IRENICISM?

It is in fact quite important for purposes of this chapter and those which follow that we get clear on this meaning of

11. Joyce, *Anglican Moral Theology*, 61.

"polemical." Joyce, for instance, suggests that, if Hooker is indeed passionately engaged in an argument, this discredits the claim of Torrance Kirby that the *Laws* in any way represents "an irenical appeal to the hearts and minds and minds of the disciplinarian-Puritan opponents of the Elizabethan Settlement," or that Hooker can seriously be claiming to share a theological commitment to the Reformed tradition. His polemicism, she argues, shows that he has no interest in a reconciliation with the Puritans.

This, however, to misunderstand the definition of polemics, and of irenics. Irenicism, although oriented toward peace, is not necessarily about compromise. It is about unity in truth, for it understands that without truth, any peace will be unstable; this at least was how sixteenth-century thinkers saw the matter. Thus even when irenicism is the end goal of a debate, it can rarely do without some resort (often very considerable resort) to polemics, in order to show both the opponent himself, and also the undecided spectators and readers, just how serious the errors in question are. There is thus no contradiction in claiming that Hooker uses polemical means in the pursuit of a largely irenical end; i.e., that he really would like, if possible, to convince many of his Puritan opponents, that "the present form of Church government which the laws of this land have established, is such, as no law of God, nor reason of man hath hitherto alleged of force sufficient to prove they do ill, who to the uttermost of their power withstand the alteration thereof" (Pref. 1.2; a fairly modest thesis, in fact). Nor does he appear to have been delusional in such a goal; on the contrary, the reign of King James, shortly after Hooker's death, was, for all its problems, characterized by a remarkable lack of conflict and a remarkable degree of cooperation between puritans and conformist churchmen.[12]

12. See for instance the remarkably positive picture of this period

It would, to be sure, impact our reading of Hooker somewhat if we found that he took pleasure in cutting down his opponents just for fun, beyond what was needed for the purposes of his argument, or if we found that he wanted to win the argument at all costs, even if it meant consciously misrepresenting and slandering his opponents. Indeed, if this were so, it would seriously undermine his claim, in the Preface to the Laws, that "it is no part of my secret meaning to draw you hereby into hatred or to set upon the face of this cause any fairer glass, than the naked truth doth afford: but my whole endeavor is to resolve the conscience, and to show as near as I can what in this controversy the heart is to think, if it will follow the light of sound and sincere judgment" (Pref. 7.1). This claim of Hooker's is in fact quite fundamental to the task he sets himself, in distinction from his predecessors, to the structure of the *Laws*, and to his theological anthropology, in which he argues that human obedience to laws must be a willing and rational obedience. To merely beat the opponent into submission, by fair means or foul, as Joyce and others have charged him with, would appear to defeat this whole purpose. But this, as we have seen, is just the charge that such critics have not really proven. There is no doubt, to be sure, that Hooker sometimes overstates his case or misrepresents his opponents, or puts an uncharitable construction on their words; there are plenty of examples of all of these in the *Laws*. But then again, the same could be said of almost any work of polemical theology, popular or academic, even today.

After all the insightful rhetorical analyses and literary criticism of recent decades, then, there appears to be little reason to modify the old judgment that Hooker represents an impressive model, often worthy of imitation, on how to carry out theological controversy: seeking to persuade

---

documented in Fincham, *Prelate as Pastor.*

without compromising, passionately opposed to error, but patient in uncovering it, formidable without being a bully. Having conceded then in this chapter that Hooker certainly does not float above history but is ready to get down and fight in the trenches of theological and political polemic, we will turn in the next chapter to consider the ways in which he nonetheless is able to transcend that immediate context with philosophical reflection of enduring relevance.

FOR DISCUSSION

1. How does Hooker use shifts of rhetorical tone in his Preface to both appeal to and denigrate his adversaries?
2. What are some problems with A. J. Joyce's reading of Hooker's polemical method?
3. How might Hooker's irenical intent and polemical method be reconciled?

6

HOOKER AS PHILOSOPHER

RECONCILING HEAVEN AND EARTH

ONE OF THE LAST, but certainly not the least, of the criticisms which *A Christian Letter* hurls at Hooker is that he has left the pure teaching of the Scriptures for the darkness of "school divinity":

> Now in all your books, although we find many good things, many truths and fine points bravely handled, yet in all your discourse, for the most part, Aristotle the patriarch of Philosophers (with diverse other human writers) and the ingenuous schoolmen, almost in all points have some finger; Reason is highly set up against holy Scripture. . . . Do you mean to bring in a confusion of all things, to reconcile heaven and earth, and to make all religions equal? Will you bring us to Atheism, or to Popery?[1]

Now we have already seen that Hooker has no interest in returning to popery, and as for atheism, he in fact goes out of his way to attack it in several passages of the Laws.

1. FLE 4:65–68.

But the anonymous critic was not simply imagining things when it came to Hooker's reliance on Aristotle and the medieval scholastics. In Book I, especially, we may spot their influence on almost every page: in chapter 2 he cites Homer, Hermes Trismegistus, Anaxagoras, Plato, the Stoics, and Boethius; in chapter 3, Aristotle and his student Theophrastus, Hippocrates, Pseudo-Dionysius, and Aquinas; in chapter 4, Orpheus and again Aristotle; in chapters 5 and 6, Plato once, Trismegistus twice, and Aristotle twice; indeed, chapter 6 contains an aside on the advantages of Aristotelian logic over the recently-developed Ramist system. This density of classical and scholastic citations continues throughout Book I, and although it drops off a fair bit thereafter, no attentive reader can fail to be impressed by it.[2]

The author of *A Christian Letter* was thus only the first in a long line to marvel at Hooker's debt to Aristotle (whom Hooker called "the arch-philosopher" [I.10.4]) and Aquinas (whom he called "the greatest amongst the school-divines" [III.9.2]), and to seek to drive a wedge between this scholastic method and the pure gospel of the Reformers.[3] Some have followed in the *Letter*'s footsteps to raise this as a criticism of Hooker's rationalism, while many others have praised him for it, seeing in this an advance beyond the supposed anti-intellectualism and primitivism of the magisterial Reformers,

---

2. For a full survey, see McGrade, "Classical, Patristic, and Medieval Sources."

3. By "scholastic method" here, I mean the attempt to rationally organize the study of theology by means of the application of rigorous philosophical distinctions, and also, more often than not, to relate the knowledge gained by revelation with the knowledge available to reason, as testified in the writings of pre-Christian philosophers, especially Aristotle. The first heyday of scholasticism was the period c. 1100–1350 in the medieval Catholic church, but the method flourished in both Protestant and Catholic contexts again from c. 1560–1700.

a key pillar of the new "Anglican" edifice that Hooker was building.

However, in twentieth-century Reformed historical theology there arose a recognition that in fact a great many Reformed theologians in the late sixteenth and early seventeenth century could be seen returning to Aristotle, to Aquinas, and to scholastic method in general. Initially the reaction to this recognition was not unlike *A Christian Letter*'s, with advocates of the "Calvin against the Calvinists" thesis decrying the Reformed scholastics' betrayal of the original biblical and humanistic impulse of the early Reformers.[4] More recently, Richard Muller and other scholars have led a full-fledged assault on this historiography, demonstrating that scholastic method, respect for Aristotelian philosophy, and extensive appropriation of the Thomistic tradition especially were commonplace among the Reformers.[5] However, even right up through some of the most recent publications, most Hooker scholars have remained seemingly unaware of this debate, with A. J. Joyce continuing to set Hooker's Thomism and Aristotelianism over against his claim to continuity with the Reformers.[6] While one can certainly find passages from Luther and Calvin critiquing Aristotle and the scholastics, many other Reformers did not share this prejudice, and this becomes increasingly so as we reach the third and fourth generation of Protestant theologians, Hooker's contemporaries.

That said, it has been hard for readers of Hooker to shake off the nagging sense that there is something different

---

4. See for instance Armstrong, *Calvinism and the Amyraut Heresy.*

5. Although much of Muller's corpus could be cited here, perhaps the key work is his *After Calvin.*

6. See especially 72–93. For a fine counterpoint to such claims, see Paul Dominiak's forthcoming essay, "Hooker, Scholasticism, and Reformed Orthodoxy."

about his philosophical method, something perhaps a little too humanistic (in the modern sense) or rationalistic. C. S. Lewis speaks for many when he observes, "Sometimes a suspicion crosses our mind that the doctrine of the Fall did not loom quite large enough in his universe."[7] For Hooker in the *Laws*, the emphasis is rarely, as for so many of the Reformers a few decades before, or for his Puritan contemporaries, upon the radical effacement of human intellectual and moral capacity that the fall precipitated. Rather, he prefers to emphasize just how much of man's created abilities have been left to him even in his fallen state, an emphasis that he finds in Aquinas as well, and which gives both of them confidence to make extensive use of Aristotle and other pagan philosophers in outlining natural theology, natural law, and logical method. To be sure, Hooker's robust doctrines of natural theology (which we shall treat briefly below) and natural law (which we shall look at in chapter 9) find parallels in the work of many of his Reformed predecessors and contemporaries. But still, shouldn't we expect him to say more about sin and its debilitating effects?

Well, perhaps not necessarily. Part of readers' puzzlement on this score derives from the attempt to treat the *Laws* as much more of a systematic theology than it ever claims to be. While as we have already seen, and shall see much more, elements of systematic theology can be found throughout, Hooker never claimed to be writing more than a defence of the civil laws governing the church of England; it was for him more a book of politics than of what we would call theology. When we compare, for instance, Book I of the *Laws* with the somewhat similar works of his contemporaries, Junius's *De Politiae* and Althusius's *Politica* and *Dicaeologica*, we find if anything *less* mention of sin and fall in their treatises than his. Meanwhile, Hooker's more

7. *English Literature*, 461.

explicitly theological writings, in the sermons and tractates, contain clear and forceful articulations of human depravity and sinfulness. Indeed, even in the *Laws,* he concludes his exposition of the law of reason (what Aquinas called the "natural law") with two strong provisos.

First,

> I deny not but lewd and wicked custom, beginning perhaps at the first amonst few, afterwards spreading into greater multitudes, and so continuining from time to time, may be of force even in plain things to smother the light of natural understanding, because men will not bend their wits to examine, whether things wherewith they have been accustomed, be good or evil.

Second,

> whatsoever we have hitherto taught, or shall hereafter, concerning the force of man's natural understanding, this we always desire withal to be understood, that there is no kind of faculty or power in man or any other creature, which can rightly perform the functions allotted to it, without perpetual aid and concurrence of that supreme cause of all things. The benefit whereof as oft as we cause God in his justice to withdraw, there can no other thing follow, than that which the Apostle noteth, even men endued with the light of reason to walk notwithstanding "in the vanity of their mind, having their cogitations darkened." (I.8.11)

That said, Hooker certainly does have a tendency in the *Laws* to always look on the bright side, whether in discussing what the fallen mind can naturally know of God and his laws, or in expounding the potential benefits of a rather dubious set of church administrative policies, or in expressing his confidence that, if there is anything seriously amiss, the governing authorities will not be slow to hear and respond appropriately.

Hooker's approach to human reason, however, rests on more than a mere habitual optimism; in fact, it derives from his allegiance to the Thomistic dictum that *grace does not destroy nature, but perfects it*.[8] This famous formula is never stated in so many words in the *Laws*, but the principle is clearly operative, and Hooker's own formulation of it is perhaps even more lucid: "the . . . Apostle teacheth . . . that nature hath need of grace, whereunto I hope we are not opposite, by holding that grace hath use of nature" (III.8.6). Let us unpack this statement, one half at a time.

NATURE HATH NEED OF GRACE

When Hooker says that "nature hath need of grace," he does not merely have in mind fallen human nature's desperate need for the redemption promised in Christ. To be sure, this is affirmed unequivocally in the *Laws*, but this need is so pressing precisely because mankind is meant for life in God. All created things, says Hooker, following an Aristotelian metaphysic, strive by nature not merely toward particular goods, but to a comprehensive final good, "our sovereign *good* or *blessedness*, that wherein the highest degree of all our perfection consisteth, that which being once attained unto there can rest nothing further to be desired" (I.11.1). And since "there can be no goodness desired which proceedeth not from God himself, as from the supreme cause of all things," it is clear that "all things in the world are said in some sort to seek the highest, and to covet more or less the particiation of God himself" (I.5.2). Although

---

8. See Neelands, "Scripture, Reason, and 'Tradition,'" 76–89, for a good discussion of Hooker in relation to this Thomistic dictum.

this is true of all creatures, it is especially true of mankind, the capstone of creation, who is capable of participating in God by his reason and will, knowing God and loving him: "Then are we happy therefore when fully we enjoy God, as an object wherein the powers of our souls are satisfied even with everlasting delight: so that although we be men, yet by being unto God united we live as it were the life of God" (I.11.2).

Now this desire for supernatural happiness, Hooker is at pains to establish, is itself *natural*, for all men have it. It is not in our power *not* to desire this, he says. Therefore, being naturally desired, it must in some sense within natural capacity since "It is an axiom of nature that natural desire cannot utterly be frustrate" (I.11.4). So man's reason is not enclosed within the bounds of creation, but naturally transcends these bounds, by desiring and striving unto the supernatural end of union with God.

Of course, Hooker has no doubt that, fallen as we are, we have lost this natural capacity for the supernatural, but we have not lost the desire, nor have we lost all knowledge of the object of this desire. On the contrary, Hooker is convinced, with Paul in Romans 1, that unbelievers are still dimly aware of it, and that the greatest amongst pagan philosophers succeeded in discerning many fundamental truths about God as the supreme source of being and governor of the world. At their best, says Hooker, they have been able to recognize our creaturely dependence on Him, and to discern such duties as "that in all things we go about his aid is by prayer to be craved," and "that he cannot have sufficient honour done unto him, but the utmost of that we can do to honour him we must" (I.8.7, quoting Plato's *Timaeus* and Aristotle's *Ethics*).

This natural knowledge of and desire for God has important consequences not only for Hooker's attempt to lay out the foundations of natural law in Book I of the *Laws*, but throughout his defense of the English Church. Although we often think of liturgy, church government, and all the rest falling within some self-contained bubble of "grace" over against "nature" or "redemption" over against creation, Hooker recognizes that nothing could be further from the case. On the contrary, he argues, the public exercise of the Christian religion is simply the full, purified, and rightly-directed expression of this natural impulse to do "the utmost of that we can do to honour him." Christ is the fulfillment of long ages of pagan yearning, and so our worship of Christ, far from seeking to rid itself of any resemblance to non-Christian religions, should seek to adopt and perfect all that is best in them.

A great example of how this conviction informs Hooker's method can be found in his discussion of festival days and the legitimacy of the church calendar in Book V of the *Laws*. He begins with an elaborate disquisition on the nature of time, the rhythms of rest and motion appropriate to all created beings, and on God's action within created time. All of these things lead men naturally to "the sanctification of days and times" as "a token of that thankfulness and a part of that public honor which we owe to God for his admirable benefits" (V.70.1). Even heathen peoples therefore testify "that festival solemnities are a part of the public exercise of religion" (V.70.5), and besides, he adds, working his way through the church year holiday by holiday, they are of great importance to "keep us in perpetual remembrance" (V.70.8), of God's redeeming work. Therefore, "the very law of nature itself which all men confess to be God's law requireth in general no less the sanctification of times than of places, persons, and things unto God's honor" (V.70.9). Hooker follows a similar method in his discussion of matrimony a few chapters later, even going so far as to justify the appropriateness of celebrating the Eucharist within the wedding ceremony by referencing "the laws of Romulus" which "established the use of certain special solemnities, whereby the minds of men were drawn to make the greater conscience of wedlock" (V.73.8).

The same conviction undergirds Hooker's understanding of the place of religion in a political commonwealth. Rather than seeking to justify the queen's authority in the church by reference to Old Testament examples like Hezekiah and Josiah, as many of his predecessors did, Hooker begins with Aristotle:

> For of every politic society that being true which Aristotle hath, namely, "that the scope thereof is not simply to live, nor the duty so much to provide for life, as for means of living well": and that even as the soul is the worthier part of man, so human societies are much more to care for that which tendeth properly unto the soul's estate, than for such temporal things as this life doth stand in need. of. (VIII.1.4, quoting Aristotle, *Politics* III.6)

Political theology, on this understanding, is simply rightly-ordered political philosophy.[9]

GRACE HATH USE OF NATURE

From this conviction, then, that nature naturally finds its fulfillment in grace, the other half of Hooker's dictum readily follows: "grace hath use of nature." The purpose of Christian revelation is not to nullify everything we thought we knew about God, but rather to illuminate that which we already dimly perceived, and toward which we feebly

---

9. For a fuller exploration of this theme, see my essay "More than a Swineherd."

and failingly groped, lost in sin though we were. Accordingly, although faith itself is a miraculous gift from God, even faith takes root in our natural faculties of reason and will. And when we come to reflect on that faith and apply it in our lives, God calls on us to do so using these natural capacities with which he has endowed us. Hooker has little patience with those who "never use reason so willingly as to disgrace reason," concluding somehow that "the way to be ripe in faith, were to be raw in wit and judgement; as if reason were an enemy unto religion, childish simplicity the mother of ghostly and divine wisdom" (III.8.4). Grace is not an enemy to nature, God is not hostile to that which he has made. To be sure, Scripture has plenty of warnings about the vain speculations of philosophy, or prideful human attempts to use reason to sound out the depths of God, or exalt man against God. But to extend this warning to a blanket critique of the power of reason itself "were to injure even God himself, who being that light which none can approach unto, hath sent out these lights whereof we are capable, even as so many sparkles resembling the bright fountain from which they rise" (III.8.9).[10]

Hooker goes on to point out how the Apostles themselves make use of the power of rational argument to expound the meaning of the Scriptures and to refute errors; indeed, the very fact that God has revealed himself through a text, rather than by immediate mystical experience, is testimony enough that he has ordained reason "as a necessary instrument, without which we could not reap, by the scriptures perfection, that fruit and benefit which it yieldeth" (III.8.10). Hooker's frequent appeals to the careful reasoning of the medieval scholastics, and to the philosophical insights of the ancient pagans, manifests his conviction that

10. For a fuller exposition, see Kirby, "The 'sundrie waies of Wisdom.'"

"the bounds of wisdom are large, and within them much is contained" (II.1.4). Rather than summoning us to a narrow biblicism, then, true faith, illuminated by the Spirit and the Word, seeks the knowledge of God in creation and in history, in the testimony of good laws and wise men, even pagans like Aristotle.

However, we should not necessarily take this, as many readers of Hooker have, as primarily an attempt to exalt the powers of unaided reason. More often, it is a matter of lowering the bar of what constitutes sufficient assurance in most of the mundane affairs of human life. Reason cannot provide the same certainty as faith, and even while essential for adjudicating doctrinal disputes, it remains a mere instrument in the hands of faith.[11] But the certainty of faith should not be demanded in every area of life; as we saw above in his critique of the dangers of puritan biblicism, this simply leads well-meaning zealots to confuse their own opinions with the voice of God, with terrible consequences. Instead of demanding the certainty of direct revelation, we should recognize that this was rarely to be had. Accordingly, more often than not, the task of reason was, in the absence of "proof infallible," to offer "probable persuasions," and to teach us to be content to be "so far persuaded as those grounds of persuasion which are to be had will bear" (II.7.5). To do otherwise, Hooker worried, would prove the shipwreck of many anxious souls.

Hooker's philosophical method, in other words, far from betraying a penchant for lofty abstract speculation, is

---

11. Hooker has much to say about the different levels of certainty that different sources and kinds of knowledge afford us. See for instance, *Certainty and Perpetuity of Faith*, FLE 5:69–73 for his famous distinction of "certainty of evidence" and "certainty of adherence"; see also *Laws* Pref. 6.6; II.7.5 for distinctions between "probable" and "demonstrative" reasoning. Voak has a thorough analysis in *Richard Hooker and Reformed Theology*, 71–78.

often deployed in subordination to a concrete pastoral task, giving assurance to troubled consciences. Let us turn then to consider Hooker the Pastor.

FOR DISCUSSION

1. Why might Hooker's use of classical and medieval philosophy raise eyebrows among some of his readers? Should it have done so?
2. What does Hooker mean by "Nature hath need of grace"?
3. What does Hooker mean by "Grace hath use of nature"?

7

HOOKER AS PASTOR

In considering Hooker the polemicist, we noted a certain tension between what Hooker claimed to be doing and what he sometimes seemed to be doing. On the one hand, he insisted that his "whole endeavour is to resolve the conscience" of his adversaries, to bring them to a conscientious, rational understanding of their errors and of the lawfulness of those customs of the English Church that they were opposing. He has no interest, he protests, in simply winning a debate, or getting them to knuckle under and blindly obey; rather, he hopes to genuinely win them over. And yet, we saw at the same time a formidable polemical wit, not afraid to make a passing slash at his opponents or to pull the rug from under their feet, leaving them looking rather foolish and no doubt feeling indignant if not enraged. For some scholars, this incongruity is reconciled by refusing to take Hooker's protestations of irenic intent seriously, but if *persuasion* is not really the goal of the *Laws*, much of its argument would seem superfluous.

Perhaps we can better understand Hooker's polemical irenicism by considering his pastoral sensibility. The pastor, after all, is a shepherd, and as such charged with nourishing the sheep, bringing back those who have strayed, and protecting them all against wolves. Of course, the challenge for pastors in every age has been that it is not always clear who is merely a straying sheep and who is a wolf—who is to be gently but firmly led back and who is to be harshly repelled in order to protect the real sheep. Hooker's overtures to the presbyterians and precisianists as erring brothers give way at times to sharp rebukes and refutations when he thinks that either the peace of the realm or the security of souls are at stake.

Whether or not he managed his pastoral task perfectly, it does seem clear that Hooker took it seriously. Indeed, throughout his writing and ministry, we find him guided at least in large part by an earnest concern for tender souls, and by the on-the-ground practical demands of Christian living. To be sure, we have to rely for this assessment almost entirely on his writings, and his few sermons that have survived, since we have too little reliable evidence of his actual pastoral ministry to know this biographically. But his written legacy provides consistent testimony of his pastoral sensibility.

RULES, EXCEPTIONS, AND EDIFICATION

Although we have emphasized Hooker's philosophical bent, it should be clear that this was not the stereotype of the philosopher with his head in the clouds, more interested in abstract generalities than on-the-ground realities. This becomes the more clear when we observe how, in his moral philosophy in particular, he evinces a deep interest in the moral demands of the concrete and specific circumstance, of the exception and not merely the rule. Despite Hooker's preoccupation with *law*, which is by its nature a general norm that is forced to abstract from the particularities of human experience, A. J. Joyce has noted that he is just as interested, like Aristotle and Aquinas before him, in its necessary complement, *equity*. Equity was the all-important moral sensibility, arising from long experience of the world and deep knowledge of the law, that enabled a judge to recognize when something, although perhaps contrary to the letter of the law, nonetheless honored its spirit, or disclosed the limitation inherent in the law. We see this notion, and a consequent concern to carve out space for the exceptional case, repeatedly in the *Laws*, whether it be in Hooker's defense of baptism by women, non-episcopal ordination, etc.[1] His frequent objection to precisianist biblicism was that by subjecting all things to presumed universal rules from Scripture, they risked elevating the rule, in some circumstances, over the urgent spiritual needs of believers.

For instance, in the case of private baptism by midwives, which had been a common practice on occasions when newborns, dying shortly after childbirth, could not be brought to a minister in time, Hooker reproached Thomas Cartwright's hardheartedness. Cartwright had written that even if it were true that "the infants which die in baptism should be assuredly damned (which is most false) yet ought not the orders which God hath set in his Church be broken after this sort." Hooker agreed that baptism was not strictly necessary to salvation in this way, but he felt for those simple Christian mothers who nonetheless urgently desired that their children be baptized before they die, and berated Cartwright fiercely:

> O sir, you that would spurn thus at such as in case of so dreadful extremity should lie prostrate before your feet, you that would turn away your face from them at the hour of their most need, you that would dam up your ears and harden your heart as iron against the unresistable cries

---

1. See Joyce, *Anglican Moral Theology*, ch. 7, for a full exposition, and examples from the *Laws*.

> of supplicants calling upon you for mercy with terms of such invocation as that most dreadful perplexity might minister if God by miracle did open the mouths of infants to express their supposed necessity, should first imagine yourself in their case and them in yours. (V.61.4)[2]

In a more positive key, Hooker also took seriously the concrete spiritual needs of ordinary congregants in his defense of many of the disputed liturgical practices of the English church. Having first established his case for why the church should have significant freedom in developing and altering church ceremonies, rather than being strictly tied to some imagined biblical model, Hooker sought to show, in many chapters of Book V of the *Laws*, that the particular liturgy of the Church of England was especially suited to the edification of the saints. The Puritans, too, you will recall, had been very concerned with *edification*, but understood it almost exclusively in terms of preaching and teaching. For Hooker, the whole believer—mind and emotion, soul and body—was involved. "Now men are edified," he wrote,

> when either their understanding is taught somewhat whereof in such actions it behooveth all men to consider, or when their hearts are moved with any affection suitable thereunto, when their minds are in any sort stirred up unto that reverence, devotion, attention and due regard, which in those cases seemeth requisite. Because therefore unto this purpose not only speech but sundry sensible means besides have always been thought necessary, and especially those means

---

2. Another practice which Hooker defended against some Puritan complaints was that of funeral services and sermons (V.75); for a touching example of Hooker's own use of such an occasion to comfort his flock, see his sermon, *A Remedie against Sorrow and Feare* (FLE 5:363–78).

> which being object to the eye, the liveliest and the most apprehensive sense of all other, have in that respect seemed the fittest to make a deep and a strong impression. (IV.1.3)

Of course, to say that Hooker is guided by pastoral concerns in his critique of the Puritans is not to say that his opponents are simply un-pastoral. It is too easy to draw a careless contrast between the heartless, legalistic Puritan and Hooker as the salver of the tender conscience, or between a cold abstract predestinarian and Hooker's warmer, more down-to-earth perspective. To be sure, there were Puritan theologians more concerned with rules than souls, abstract logic than spiritual needs, just as there were conformist theologians more concerned with civil laws than souls, proper hierarchy than spiritual needs. But most of the time, most parties to these disputes, as to other intra-Protestant disputes then and now, took for granted that their goal was to comfort troubled souls, point them to Christ, and teach them to follow in his ways. The difference was over how best to do that.

Indeed, although Hooker might have had much to say, against the precisianists and presbyterians, about the need for biblical laws to be flexible and accommodate the exceptional case, the moderate Puritans might have asked why he did not similarly emphasize the need for civil laws to do likewise. Recall that for many of the more moderate Puritans, the concern was simply that ministers have freedom to omit ceremonies that seemed spiritually harmful to their particular flocks. While many bishops had permitted such "occasional nonconformity," Archbishop Whitgift had led a crackdown after taking office in 1583, and such flexibility was not to be reappear until a few years into the reign of King James. Hooker may well have been content to tolerate this, had he been in a position of authority, but he never really explicitly says so in the *Laws*, and often appears to treat the ecclesiastical laws of England, at least in principle, to be universally binding. For him, the political dangers of allowing individuals to decide when and when not to observe the law could trump the pastoral dangers of too little flexibility.

THE PROBLEM OF ASSURANCE

There was one pastoral challenge, however, that went much deeper than the stubborn debates about which ceremonies were more or less edifying, and which preoccupied Hooker throughout his life. This was the cluster of problems surrounding the doctrines of predestination and assurance, with which we can find nearly every Reformed theologian of Hooker's day repeatedly grappling. Indeed, this is a paradigmatic example of how debates were less over *whether* to be pastorally sensitive, but rather over which doctrines were in fact the best suited to provide comfort to troubled souls. When the Reformation began, Luther came preaching liberation to captive consciences, declaring that struggling sinners need not look despairingly at the inadequacy of their works but could rest with full comfort on Christ as their sure possession by faith. Luther himself had known the struggle for assurance as a monk, gnawed by the fear that he was among the damned and trying in vain to "make his calling and election sure" by being the most pious and ascetic monk of all. While Luther's own struggle was rather more exceptional than most, it was certainly the case that the medieval church did not put a premium on providing assurance of salvation. On the contrary, it actively resisted the idea, and a frequent Catholic critique of the Reformers was that their doctrine gave believers a false security, presumption rather than humble faith, which, by taking salvation for granted, lost all incentive to keep struggling with sin and living a holy life. Even the holiest saint, the Catholic Church taught, could never have full assurance of his salvation, since he could still fall at any point into mortal sin, and die without having reconciled himself to Christ. Faith, hope, and love must always be tempered by a healthy fear.

Against this doctrine, then, the Reformers declared that it was in fact of the essence of saving faith to be supremely confident. Since saving faith looked not to the believer's own insufficient works, but to Christ himself, the sure foundation, true faith should be free of doubting. The famous first question of the Heidelberg Catechism sums it up well:

> Q. What is your only comfort in life and in death?
>
> A. That I am not my own, but belong—body and soul, in life and in death—to my faithful Savior, Jesus Christ. He has fully paid for all my sins with his precious blood, and has set me free from the tyranny of the devil. He also watches over me in such a way that not a hair can fall from my head without the will of my Father in heaven; in fact, all things must work together for my salvation. Because I belong to him, Christ, by his Holy Spirit, assures me of eternal life and makes me wholeheartedly willing and ready from now on to live for him.

From this perspective, doubt of one's salvation was doubt of the truthfulness of Christ's promises, and hence itself a failure of faith. Doubt was then perhaps a self-fulfilling prophecy: if you worried that you weren't saved, well then, apparently you weren't. Of course, it was not quite that simple; Debora Shuger, in a fantastic essay on Hooker's doctrine of assurance, has shown that in fact the magisterial Reformers, as well as the English Puritans, could both insist that true faith was unwavering and certain, *and* insist that true faith was always assailed by doubt and would never be unwavering in this life.[3] This unstable dialectic was to lead some Protestants into the same kinds of tortures of conscience that Luther had originally sought to escape.

This was especially the case when the doctrine of true faith as sure confidence was fused with the doctrine of predestination. A strong doctrine of predestination, while certainly not original to the Reformers (and Luther was nearly as forceful on many aspects of the doctrine as Calvin), was a particular emphasis of theirs. Again, the initial impetus was to provide positive assurance of and gratitude for God's grace, over against the constant wavering and striving of the medieval saint. The believer, once he had been taken hold of by Christ, could rest assured in the doctrine of the perseverance of the elect: that God had chosen him for salvation from before the beginning of the world, and that "no one could pluck him out of His hand" (John 10:29).

One can readily see, however, how this doctrine might backfire, particularly when combined with the doctrine of the certainty of faith. If one could only know that one was of the elect by the fact of one's faith, then a doubting, wavering faith might well undermine any such confidence, and if confidence was taken to be essential, might suggest the conclusion that one was in fact reprobate. The very urgency of the issue could of course cause the problem to be self-reinforcing, with even very minor lapses of faith quickly escalating into profound fears. In response to this crisis of conscience, Reformed theologians, especially Puritans in England, began to develop a range of techniques for

3. Shuger, "Faith and Assurance."

soothing such worried souls. In particular, they exhorted believers to examine not only the quality of their faith, but the state of their lives, to see whether they were obeying all of Christ's commands and thereby displaying the fruit of true faith. Once again, one can readily see how these demands could simply exacerbate the problem and leave consciences in a state not dissimilar to that which had provoked Luther's protest to begin with. The demand for certainty just produced more and more uncertainty—many who examined their faith hoping to find it sure and stable found themselves more likely to doubt, while those who examined their works looking for sure fruit of godliness came to demand an impossibly certain standard for showing them what the will of God was.[4]

A final solution was to distract the worried believer from the uncertainty of his own faith by focusing on the clear lines that divided him from the unfaithful. By comparison to lovers of the world and papists, the Puritan could at least feel fairly good about his own spiritual state. This kind of "experimental predestinarianism" therefore could encourage zealous believers not merely to ask whether they themselves were among the elect, but whether their neighbors were. The distinction between visible and invisible church, so essential to the early Reformers, risked being blurred, as some puritans sought to draw visible lines as to which so-called Christians really were in Christ. Roman Catholics were generally written off entirely, and many lukewarm members of the Church of England, or those taken to compromise important doctrines, were immediately suspect as well.

---

4. The classic treatment of this problem was R. T. Kendall's *Calvin and English Calvinism*, although many of the larger conclusions that he draws have been hotly disputed. See also, however, the careful studies of Brachlow, *Communion of Saints*, and Bozeman, *Precisianist Strain*.

THE SAFEST AXIOMS FOR CHARITY

From Hooker's first sermons at the Temple Church in 1585 until his last published writings, we find him struggling to overcome these problematic turns within much English theology, to "resolve the consciences" of his hearers not by providing some infallibly certain rule to judge the state of consciences, but by encouraging them to accept the reality of uncertainty and live within its limits. I want to look briefly at his response to the last problem we just mentioned—the temptation to think that we could know when other people were *not* among the elect—before considering his approach to the subjective problem—how can I know that *I* am?

Hooker's great hesitation to make judgments concerning the salvation of others reflected the policy of his monarch, Elizabeth I, who is said to have declared, "I would not open windows into men's souls." But Hooker went further than mere agnosticism, insisting that our duty is, in the absence of unambiguous evidence to the contrary, to assume that all those who profess Christ are genuinely his. He states his principle with admirable crispness at one point in the *Laws*:

> Howbeit concerning the state of all men with whom we live, we may till the world's end, for the present, always presume, that as far as in us there is power to discern what others are, and as far as any duty of ours dependeth upon the notice of their condition in respect of God, the safest axioms for charity to rest it self upon are these, "He which already believeth is; and He which believeth not as yet may be the child of God." (V.49.2)

The doctrine of predestination, although asserting that some are indeed irrevocably bound for damnation, never gives us license, argues Hooker, to rejoice in this fact or try to determine which of those around us are among their number, as some of his contemporaries were tempted to do. For all we know, any given human being now living could be one of the elect, so we ought to pray for and seek the salvation of each.

But Hooker extends this rule of charity elsewhere to insist that we must, as far as any duty of ours depends on the matter, not only assume that whoever "already believeth," but also whoever *professes belief* is already a child of God. This, of course, many of his Puritan contemporaries would hotly dispute. It is manifest, they would say, that many professing Christians do not live like Christians, and it is the task of the church to judge hypocrites and cast them out. Such an aggressive policy of church discipline was at the heart of the presbyterian reform agenda. Hooker is not opposed to any church discipline, but he is exceedingly wary about claims to know men's eternal state, and wary about raising too high the bar of admission into the kingdom.

Hooker accordingly presents a very minimalist account of the bounds of the visible church, and a relatively minimalist account of the bounds of the invisible. Of the former, he insists that profession of faith and baptism only are needed to count one as a member of the visible church, even if one's wicked behavior or false doctrine clearly contradicts this profession; these simply mean that one is, to all appearances, an unfaithful member, but a member still, and one who may yet revive and bear fruit. We will elaborate on this important argument in chapter 10, on Hooker's ecclesiology, but what about the latter issue—the minimalist account of the bounds of the invisible church?

It was this which led Hooker to say, in a sermon at the Temple, "I doubt not that God was merciful to save thousands of our fathers living in popish superstitions, in as much as they sinned ignorantly," thus provoking the wrath of his subordinate Walter Travers. Hooker responded to Travers's accusations in a series of meticulously-argued sermons which were later published as *A Learned Discourse of Justification, Works, and How the Foundation of Faith is Overthrown*.[5] Although this treatise contains a wonderful exposition of the respective Protestant and Catholic doctrines on faith and works, the key point of dispute is identified by the subtitle. What is the "foundation of faith"? And how is it "overthrown"?

Hooker's point, though densely argued, can be summed up well in a phrase that one sometimes hears nowadays: "We are justified by faith in Christ alone, not justified by faith in justification by faith alone." In other words, Jesus Christ as our only Lord and Savior is the object of the Christian's faith, the foundation on which all else is built. It is Christ who saves, not the strength or precision of our faith. That is not to say that the doctrine of justification by faith is unimportant; on the contrary, the Catholic rejection of it does in fact overthrow the foundation by logical consequence. But so do many errors, including, notes Hooker, the Lutheran doctrine of the ubiquity of Christ's body. But the Reformed do not thereby consider Lutherans to be apostate. Just so, he says, a great many Catholic laymen and clergy lived and died confessing Jesus Christ as their only Savior, not perceiving the contradiction between their profession and their doctrine, and upon such God can and does have mercy. He concludes his final sermon on this with a passionate peroration that has justly earned fame as one of Hooker's finest passages:

> Let me die if ever it be proved, that simply an error doth exclude a Pope or a Cardinal in such a case utterly from hope of life. Surely I must confess unto you, if it be an error to think that

5. The standard critical edition can be found in *FLE* 5:105–69.

God may be merciful to save men, even when they err, my greatest comfort is my error. Were it not for the love I bear unto this error, I would neither wish to speak nor to live.[6]

GOD IS GREATER THAN OUR HEARTS

Hooker, as we have seen, is thus keen to lower the threshold of what should count as sufficient *content of faith* in order for faith to be genuine and saving. So we should not be surprised to see him doing something similar with regard to the *certainty of faith*. In fact, the sermon where Hooker treats this issue, *A Learned and Comfortable Sermon of the Certainty and Perpetuity of Faith in the Elect*,[7] another of the very few that survive, appears to have been preached a few weeks before the sermons on justification. Here he grapples squarely with the problem of assurance that we discussed above. Many Protestants, as we saw, were very reluctant to say that saving faith could be uncertain. After all, didn't that imply doubt in the promises or power of God? Hooker's solution, which appears to us in retrospect quite obvious, once again proved quite controversial at the time.

In his sermon, he drew upon a set of distinctions articulated by both Aristotle and Aquinas, regarding the relation between the objects of our knowledge and the nature of our knowledge. As Debora Shuger summarizes, "There exists an inverse proportion between the excellence of an object and its knowability: the more excellent the object, the less knowable to us."[8] Thus I can readily know, standing in a garden, that I see a rose in front of me; indeed, by careful investigation, I can arrive at a very detailed and con-

6. FLE 5:165.

7. The standard critical edition can be found in *FLE* 5:69–82.

8. Shuger, "Faith and Assurance," 236.

fident knowledge of that rose's anatomy. And yet this rose is very lowly on the order of being: it will soon wither and die, and I can have no confidence that because it is there today, it will be there tomorrow. On the other hand, divine realities, eternal and utterly certain in themselves, I can know only dimly and shakily. Hooker accordingly notes that our minds naturally assent or withhold assent based on the degree of evidence they perceive:

> Certainty of evidence we call that, when the mind doth assent unto this or that; not because it is true in itself, but because the truth thereof is clear, because it is manifest unto us. Of things in themselves most certain, except they be also most evident, our persuasion is not so assured as it is of things more evident although in themselves they be less certain.[9]

Jesus Christ is more sure than any earthly thing, and yet, whereas every one of us knows unproblematically that roses exist, many people do not know Christ. Is our knowledge of him only a matter of vague opinion, then, as critics of Christianity would say? No, says Hooker, for this shortfall in "certainty of evidence" is made up for by the "certainty of adherence," in which our spirits, "having once truly tasted the heavenly sweetness" of Christ, cling fast to him even in the midst of doubt or contrary evidence: the believer "striveth with himself to hope even against hope to believe even against all reason of believing."[10]

But this in itself does not resolve the problem, does it? Hooker has shifted the weight from the cognitive dimension to the affective dimension, but a Puritan attached to the importance of assurance could still readily retort, "If

9. *FLE* 5:70.
10. *FLE* 5:71.

those who truly know and love Christ adhere to him by a love that transcends knowledge, then those who doubt and waver in this love show themselves not to be saved." The remainder of Hooker's sermon seeks to deny that this conclusion follows, and in it he shows some of his greatest pastoral sensitivity and eloquence.

In the sermon he is considering the prophet Habakkuk's despairing lament, "the law fails, and judgment goes not forth" (1:4). This certainly looks like a lapse of faith, or at least a lapse of certainty in the prophet's faith, but does such a lapse doom the prophet? No, says Hooker. For all those who trust in Christ Jesus, "their faith when it is at the strongest is but weak, yet even then when it is at the weakest so strong that utterly it never faileth, it never perisheth altogether no not in them who think it extinguished in themselves."[11] For even when we shrink away from God, he does not shrink away from us; as 1 John puts it so memorably, in words that might well sum up Hooker's sermon, "For whenever our heart condemns us, God is greater than our hearts" (1 John 3:20).

We must not be quick to judge the doubting, says Hooker, because which of us is not among them? "The prophet's case is the case of many," observes Hooker, and goes on to diagnose the various forms that such spiritual doubt may take (including, it would seem, clinical depression: "a melancholy passion . . . the cause whereof is in the body"[12]). None of this proves that our faith is lost, for, Hooker observes, to worry that one has lost one's faith is in itself proof that one hasn't. Suppose, he says, these doubters really have lost faith.

---

11. *FLE* 5:74.
12. *FLE* 5:73, 74.

> But are they not grieved with their unbelief? They are. Do they not wish it might and also strive that it may be otherwise? We know they do. Whence cometh this but from a secret love and liking which they have of those things that are believed? No man can love the things which in his own opinion are not. And if they think those things to be, which they show that they love when they desire to believe then, then must it needs be that by desiring to believe they prove themselves to be true believers.[13]

In other words, although the cognitive dimension of their faith may have wavered, as one might expect given the lack of certainty of evidence, even to worry about such a thing shows that they still adhere to Christ, and if they continue to stubbornly do so, says Hooker, he will reward this faith with renewed certainty. Again, Hooker's concluding lines deserve quotation in full:

> I know in whom I have believed, I am not ignorant whose precious blood hath been shed for me, I have a shepherd full of kindness, full of care, and full of power; unto him I commit myself; his own finger hath engravened this sentence in the tables of my heart, "Satan hath desired to winnow thee as wheat, but I have prayed that thy faith fail not." Therefore the assurance of my hope I will labor to keep as a jewel unto the end and by labor through the gracious mediation of his prayer I shall keep it.[14]

Hooker's solution to the problem of certainty, then, when it comes to the assurance of salvation, is to accept that our frail minds often lack the certainty we wish for. To go

---

13. *FLE* 5:76.
14. *FLE* 5:82.

on demanding that we have a certainty that, in the nature of the case, we may not, will simply multiply doubts. Certainly we should not pretend that saving faith should be as easy and evident as sense-perception. Rather, we must make do with the kind of certainty that our frail faith provides, and trust that God will not let us down. I have highlighted this approach to the problem of assurance because it sums up Hooker's approach to certainty, and "resolving the conscience," on every issue. We noted above that many Puritans sought assurance of salvation not merely in the quality of their faith but even in the quality of their works, as the fruit of that faith. This laid a heavy burden on the believer's need to know the will of God in every area of life, to have "certainty of welldoing," a certainty that many Puritans would argue could come only from Scripture. Here too, Hooker worried that demanding too much certainty would simply create further uncertainty, shipwrecking souls in the mists of doubt. To expound his answer to this problem, however, we must turn to consider his doctrine of Scripture.

FOR DISCUSSION

1. Why did the Reformers emphasize the need for assurance of salvation? Why might this have been counterproductive?
2. How does Hooker think we should approach the question of others' salvation?
3. How does Hooker think we should approach the question of our own salvation?

8

KEY THEMES: SCRIPTURE

THE RELIGION OF PROTESTANTS

"The Bible, I say, the Bible only is the religion of Protestants."[1] So wrote English Protestant apologist William Chillingworth in 1637, but the same words might just as well have been written in 1537 or 1937. From the beginning of the Reformation, built on the "formal principle" of *sola Scriptura*, to the present, the Bible has remained at the center of the Protestant confession, distinguishing it from the Eastern Orthodox and Catholic faiths, with their willingness to put more weight on the role of tradition. Indeed, one might fairly argue that, if anything, the Bible has come to occupy a *more* and *more* central role in many expressions of Protestantism, particularly in the United States.

In the nineteenth century, American theologian John Nevin decried the epidemic of "private judgment" that led a whole string of would-be religious reformers to establish new sects founded, as they fervently insisted, upon the Bible alone, freeing it from the layers of superstition and

---

1. *The Religion of Protestants a Safe Way to Salvation*, 460.

confusion that centuries of interpretation had added. Ironically, though, the unshakeable faith in Scripture's comprehensiveness, simplicity, and perspicuity was on the rise just at the same time that the latest developments in scholarship were undermining such faith. With the rise of higher criticism in the late 1800s, theological liberalism took it more and more for granted that the Bible could not simply be trusted to give us everything our religion required. It must be supplemented, and often deconstructed, with critical reason. In response to the rise of liberalism, the ordinary rank-and-file of the American churches, along with a few of their more conservative leaders, doubled down on their faith in Scripture, insisting that the Bible, interpreted according to its plain "literal" sense, could tell us everything we needed or even wanted to know—the date the earth began, the date it would end, and everything in between. Contemporary Protestantism remains bitterly divided between such biblicistic fundamentalists, confessionalists who interpret their Bibles through the lens of various theological traditions, and liberals who continue to demand a wide berth for critical reason, while minimizing the ongoing authority of Scripture.

In the context of such strife, it should be no surprise that we find Richard Hooker again in the midst of the tug-of-war. On the one hand, some see in Hooker, with his attacks on Puritan biblicism, a great champion for the cause of contemporary liberalism, an enemy of fundamentalists in every age. Don H. Compier, in a short, rather insubstantial, but wonderfully representative essay, stakes such a claim:

> Following Hooker's example, we would do well to avoid modes of moral persuasion which either consist of the bare quotation of chapters and verses from Scripture, or of appeals to the inviolable authority of private conscience. . . .

> Persons in community are challenged to engage in the difficult human labor of dialogue, with Scripture and one another, in search of that communal consensus (ever revisable in new circumstances), which alone can offer a reliable enough basis for action on behalf of the common good.[2]

On the other hand, Nigel Atkinson has staked a claim on Hooker for contemporary evangelical Anglicanism, insisting that his doctrine of Scripture and scriptural authority is in all material points as strong as Calvin's.[3] Many others have, as with so many areas of Hooker's thought, claimed him as a sort of "Goldilocks" theologian—"not too hot, not too cold, but just right." This is perhaps accurate, but hopelessly vague, and can mean many different things to different people.

For instance, it has long been fashionable to claim Hooker as the founder of that quintessential Anglican compromise, the "three-legged stool" of Scripture, reason, and tradition. Of course, the notion of the three-legged stool, or "Anglican tripod," has been extensively criticized, since these three authorities don't function in at all the same way.[4] For the Protestant, Scripture is the sole source of authoritative revelation, but tradition and reason are both essential to its interpretation and application; moreover, both have an important role in deciding matters that Scripture itself leaves indifferent. This is certainly how Hooker sees the matter, though we should add that whereas for the modern, "reason" is the individual's critical judgment standing apart from the received wisdom of "tradition," for Hooker, the

---

2. Compier, "Hooker on the Authority of Scripture," 259.

3. Atkinson, *Richard Hooker and the Authority of Scripture, Reason, and Tradition.*

4. See for instance N. T. Wright, *The Last Word*, 100–102.

two are closely intertwined. To be authoritative and reliable, reason must usually have a corporate dimension, reflecting the shared wisdom of the leaders of church or state; "tradition," then, is simply the ongoing deposit of such corporate reason, exercised over centuries of Christian reflection, and requiring creative appropriation in every new generation.[5]

Certainly, however, whatever modern readers of Hooker have sometimes gotten wrong in their attempts to draw him into contemporary disputes, they have not been wrong to consider him relevant. On the contrary, I think Hooker has a great deal to offer, whether to theological conservatives who sometimes discredit their cause by making greater claims for Scripture than it can bear, or to liberals, who, recognizing that Scripture is not self-interpreting, fail to make the necessary distinctions between matters of faith and matters of practice, essentials and things indifferent. The best way to appropriate Hooker, however, is first to understand him, and the best way to understand him is to grasp his historical context.

I have referred a few times now to "things indifferent," or *adiaphora* as the Reformers called them. To understand Hooker's doctrine of Scripture, it is essential to understand the backdrop of this hotly-disputed concept.[6] One of the difficulties with the concept was that it sometimes related to the material principle of the Reformation—justification *sola fide*—and sometimes to the formal—*sola Scriptura*. That is, Luther, for instance, could talk of all works whatsoever as in one sense "indifferent"—in themselves neither meritorious or damning, but depending entirely on the faith of the doer. More often, though, Protestants spoke of those things

5. For a good discussion of Hooker's understanding of "tradition" in this regard, see Avis, *In Search of Authority*, 117–20.

6. The best treatment remains that of Verkamp, *Indifferent Mean*. See also ch. 2 of my forthcoming *Freedom of a Christian Commonwealth*.

neither commanded nor forbidden in Scripture as "indifferent"; obviously, though, something that was commanded in Scripture could still be, from one perspective, "indifferent" in Luther's sense, even if it was important to sanctification. For Luther, in other words, the stress was laid on "certainty of salvation," which we discussed in the last chapter, and which he took to be independent of works, and to be so secure that from it flowed the "certainty of welldoing" that we mentiond there in closing—the confidence that our works pleased God. Some later Protestants, especially the English Puritans, were not so sure, and insisted that Scripture only could supply such "certainty of welldoing" (without which, perhaps, there could not even be certainty of salvation, since true faith was knowable by its good fruits). Let us observe this transition more closely.

GRASPING AT STRAWS

Early in his *Treatise on Good Works*, Martin Luther writes,

> Now every one can note and tell for himself when he does what is good or what is not good; for if he finds his heart confident that it pleases God, the work is good, even if it were so small a thing as picking up a straw. If confidence is absent, or if he doubts, the work is not good, although it should raise all the dead and the man should give himself to be burned. This is the teaching of St. Paul, Romans xiv: 'Whatsoever is not done of or in faith is sin.' For all other works a heathen, Jew, a Turk, a sinner may also do; but to trust firmly that he pleases God, is possible only for a Christian who is enlightened and strengthened by grace.[7]

---

7. *Treatise on Good Works*, 25.

Faced with the age-old question, "How can I please God?" Luther answers it before he ever begins describing good works, as if to say simply: "Believe in Christ, and you will have full confidence of God's favor." Rather than flowing toward salvation, as a way of justifying the troubled conscience, good works were to flow from salvation, issuing out of a justified conscience. This proclamation was at the heart of Luther's doctrine of Christian liberty, which could be taken to render all outward works simply indifferent, so that Luther would write in the treatise that "in faith all works become equal" and it is faith alone which is the only good work. But in proclaiming all works but faith *adiaphora* in this soteriological context, Luther of course never meant to say that it didn't matter whether one did them or not, but only that the justified conscience, confident of its standing before God, did not need to focus on the value of the work itself, but could instead obey spontaneously and unconditionally.

It soon became clear, however, that even if we wanted to obey spontaneously, we still often needed a good deal of guidance as to what good works looked like in general. Indeed, most of Luther's *Treatise on Good Works* is spent expounding the Ten Commandments as a faithful summary of which sorts of things are good works and which are bad works. Within the context of describing the shape of the believer's response to God, the life of sanctification, the concept of *adiaphora* took on the latter meaning we noted above—things neither commanded nor forbidden by Scripture. Of course, it would seem that there might be things that fell within this latter sense of *adiaphora* that were still not indifferent in the full sense, as we might mean the term—plenty of morally weighty actions not addressed with any specificity in Scripture (though certainly they might be subsumed under general headings like "love your neighbor"). Accordingly, the magisterial reformers were happy to draw upon the medieval natural law tradition, as a way of reasoning about morality that did not always depend on Scripture.[8]

But natural law was vague, and vagueness would hardly do if you were struggling with the assurance of your salvation, as we noted many Protestants of Hooker's time were. If true faith necessarily did good works, then presumably one could turn around the syllogism, and reason back from the existence of good works in the life of a believer to the presence of true saving faith. But this made it all the more urgent to know just what counted as true Christian obedience; substantial gray areas of *adiaphora* simply confused matters.

At the same time, the reordering of authority caused by the Reformation served to multiply moral uncertainties in the life of the believer. No longer could the pope tell you for certain when you should and shouldn't obey your civil authorities. Accordingly, clashes of loyalty and conflicts of conscience were sure to abound, especially as civil authorities began to make use of their new freedom to legislate in adiaphora, whether civil or ecclesiastical. Were clerical vestments indifferent, or not? What about kneeling at communion? Edward and Elizabeth, royal governors of the church of England, had deemed they were, and issued legislation accordingly. But some of their subjects weren't so sure. Faced with the need to find a certain rule to adjudicate such crises of conscience, many Puritans leaned more heavily on *sola Scriptura*. If Scripture provides the church all that is necessary, and it is necessary for us to know how to obey God in all things, then it must be the case that, as leading Elizabethan puritan Thomas Cartwright so succinctly put it, "the word of God containeth the direction of

---

8. See for instance Grabill, *Rediscovering the Natural Law*.

all things pertaining to the church, *yea, of whatsoever things can fall into any part of man's life.*"[9] Protestant confessions had always taught that "Holy Scripture containeth all things necessary *to salvation*" (so begins the sixth of the Thirty-Nine Articles) but the erosion of the qualifier threatened to invert the logic of the article entirely. Instead of concluding that no one could be required to believe something beyond Scripture, as the article goes on to say, Cartwright's position held that the church was required not to do anything beyond Scripture.[10]

Again, the goal in this was to provide greater assurance to the believer, a sure rule for knowing that God was well-pleased with him. But Cartwright's route to such assurance, while hitting on some of the same themes as Luther's, turned out to be crucially different. Like Luther, he concludes that "no man's authority . . . can bring any assurance unto the conscience." Perhaps in "human sciences" the word of man carried "some small force" but "in divine matters [it] hath no force at all."[11] When pressed, however, Cartwright would expand "divine matters" to include *all* actions of moral weight, insisting that unless "have the word of God go before us in all our actions . . . we cannot otherwise be assured that they please God."[12] Why? Because "no man can glorify God in anything but by obedience; and there is no obedience but in respect of the commandment and word of God: therefore it followeth that the word of God directeth a man in all his actions."[13] Cartwright goes

9. Cartwright, *Replie*, 14 (*Whitgift's Works* 1:190).

10. Few discussions of this inversion are as lucid and to-the-point as Walter Lowrie's in *The Church and Its Organization*, 64–67.

11. Cartwright, *Second Replie*, 19.

12. Ibid. 61.

13. Cartwright, *Replie*, 14 (*Whitgift's Works* I:190), reiterated in *Second Replie*, 59.

on to quote, as Luther had done in the context of this same question, Romans 14:23, "Whatsoever is not of faith is sin." But the meaning has shifted dramatically, for as Cartwright explains, faith now means careful attendance to the commands of Scripture. Accordingly, good works no longer flow *from* assurance, but *toward* assurance. When Cartwright's interlocutor John Whitgift, perhaps noticing the parallel (or allusion?) to Luther's argument, asks whether Cartwright would extend this dependence on Scripture to any action whatsoever, even "to take up a straw,"[14] Cartwright happily swallows the *reductio*, acknowledging that in some sense the guidance of Scripture is needed for the taking up of a straw, inasmuch as, for the motive of this action to be pure, it must be part of a larger action consciously guided by adherence to the Word. From this standpoint, there really couldn't be *adiaphora* anymore—or if there were, it could only be on the basis of explicit scriptural permission, not mere scriptural silence.[15]

In order to provide the needed certainty of well doing, however, more was necessary than just a comprehensive Bible. The Bible also needed to be detailed, precise, and unambiguous wherever it provided moral guidance. As Cartwright declared, "it is the virtue of a good law to leave as little as may be in the discretion of the judge,"[16] and Scripture, as the most perfect law of all, would leave nothing to human discretion. This being the case, even where general rules of prudence would seem to be up to the job, Cartwright prefers to find a scriptural prooftext for his argument, no matter how far-fetched. For instance, when complaining that in the Prayer Book service, the minister is cannot be clearly heard by the congregation when he stands at the far end of the chancel,

---

14. *Defence of the Answere* (*Whitgift's Works* I:193).
15. Cartwright, *Second Replie*, 59.
16. *Second Replie*, appendix, i.21–22.

Cartwright invokes Acts 1:15: "Peter stood up in the midst of the disciples. . . . The place of St. Luke is an unchangeable rule to teach that all that which is done in the church ought to be done where it may be best heard, for which cause I alleged it."[17] Indeed, so far did some of these Puritans push the idea of scriptural sufficiency that they are forced to read into the texts commands that, by their own admission, aren't actually there. Thus Cartwright's colleague Walter Travers at one point argues that even though the Bible never narrates an express divine command for David and Solomon's changes to the worship and building of the temple, we know their actions would never have been approved had not such a command been given; and, since the church is even more important than Israel, we can now readily infer that the New Testament must provide such express commands for the church's liturgy.[18]

Although the primary context for these sometimes wild claims was generally church government and liturgy, there was little to stop the logic being extended into every area of life. And this, Richard Hooker realized, was pastorally disastrous.

THE END OF SCRIPTURE AND THE GROUNDS OF PERSUASION

In the last chapter, we saw how, by demanding *too much* assurance, too much certainty of salvation, many of Hooker's contemporaries were actually pushing it further and further out of reach. The same, Hooker realized, was true of the quest for certainty of welldoing. And, inasmuch as some Puritans had tied the two together, the result, he feared, would be shipwrecked consciences. If Scripture is to be our guide in

17. *Rest of the Second Replie*, 187.
18. Travers, *Full and Plaine Declaration*, 8.

everything, thus abrogating the law of nature, "what shall the scripture be but a snare and a torment to weak consciences, filling them with infinite perplexities, scrupulosities, doubts insoluble, and extreme despairs?" (II.8.6).

To be sure, there was nothing wrong with seeking certainty in principle. On the contrary, he observed, it is simply human nature: "The mind of man desireth evermore to know the truth according to the most infallible certainty which the nature of things can yield" (II.7.5). But the key phrase here was the last—*which the nature of things can yield*. The world, for all its beautiful variety and order (or perhaps *because of* its beautiful variety and order) is not a clockwork deterministic machine. It is a place full of uncertainties, possibilities, and probabilities, and it is the mark of wisdom to adapt the mode of our knowledge, and our claims to certainty, to the nature of the objects being known. Some eternal truths, he thinks, can be known intuitively and self-evidently, others by "strong and invincible demonstration." But "in case these both do fail, then which way greatest probability leadeth, thither the mind doth evermore incline" (II.7.5) Scripture too can provide us certainty in those things it clearly teaches, but not in those things that it doesn't. In fact, most of us, most of the time, rely on the probable authority of the testimony of the learned, and adjust our level of certainty accordingly. This probable assurance should suffice in most cases, so that, contra Cartwright, our consciences may be assured without direct guidance from Scripture: "In all things then are our consciences best resolved, and in most agreeable sort unto God and nature settled, when they are so farre perswaded as those grounds of perswasion which are to be had will beare." Indeed, to demand otherwise does not give greater assurance, but rather greater "perplexity":

> When bare and unbuilded conclusions are put into their minds, they finding not themselves to have thereof any great certainty, imagine that this proceedeth only from lack of faith, and that the spirit of God doth not work in them, as it doth in true believers; by this means their hearts are much troubled, they fall into anguish and perplexity: whereas the truth is, that how bold and confident soever we may be in words, when it cometh to the point of trial, such as the evidence is which the truth hath either in itself or through proof, such is the heart's assent thereunto, neither can it be stronger, being grounded as it should be. (II.7.5)

In other words, you can't make yourself more certain about something just by trying harder, if the matter is intrinsically uncertain.

So which things are uncertain, and which aren't? Hooker tried to answer these questions by providing a fresh account of both the *scope* of scriptural authority and the *mode* of scriptural authority.

Regarding the former, Hooker was resolute in affirming that Scripture was wholly sufficient "unto the end for which it was instituted." But what is this end? Well, what does Scripture itself say?

> The main drift of the whole New Testament is that which Saint John setteth down as the purpose of his own history, "These things are written, that ye might believe that Jesus is Christ the Son of God, and that in believing ye might have life through his name." The drift of the old that which the Apostle mentioneth to Timothy, "The holy Scriptures are able to make thee wise unto salvation." (I.14.4)

Accordingly, argues Hooker, everything that is necessary for our salvation in Christ must be either expressly affirmed in Scripture, or able to be readily and necessarily deduced from it (such as the doctrine of the Trinity). On the basis of this conviction, he clearly opposes the Catholic understanding of the authority of tradition, insisting that nothing essential to salvation can be added by human authority: "We utterly refuse as much as once to acquaint ourselves with any thing further. Whatsoever to make up the doctrine of man's salvation is added, as in supply of the Scripture's unsufficiency, we reject it. Scripture purposing this, hath perfectly and fully done it" (II.8.5). Whatever tradition's role in the Christian life broadly considered, for Hooker it does not even have a subordinate role when it comes to the central mysteries of the Christian faith (except in clarifying and defending the teachings of Scripture). Likewise, although Hooker insists emphatically on the value of our God-given faculty of reason, he clarifies that, "unto the word of God, being in respect of that end for which God ordained it perfect, exact, and absolute in itself, we do not add reason as a supplement of any maim or defect therein, but as a necessary instrument, without which we could not reap by the Scripture's perfection that fruit and benefit which it yieldeth" (III.8.10).

So Scripture is wholly sufficient for the end of salvation, and to this extent, Hooker believes, the Church of Rome has seriously erred. But the Puritans, he says, have erred in an equal and opposite direction, "as if Scripture did not only contain all things in that kind necessary, but all things simply, and in such sort that to do any thing according to any other law were not only unnecessary but even opposite unto salvation, unlawful and sinful" (II.8.7). This, he says, while intended as high praise for Scripture, is actually a dishonor, since God is honored only by truth, and Scripture never makes such claims for itself. This is not to say, of course, that Scripture simply has nothing at all to teach us beyond the basic truths of salvation. On the contrary, it is "stored with infinite variety of matter in all kinds" (I.14.1). Indeed, Hooker is willing to accept Cartwright's dictum that "the word of God containeth the direction of whatsoever things can fall into any part of man's life" with an important qualification. Since Scripture contains "the general axioms, rules, and principles" of the moral law, there is no reason why all moral duties might not "be deduced by some kind of consequence (as by long circuit of deduction it may be that even all truth out of any truth may be concluded)"; however, "no man [is] bound in such sort to deduce all his actions out of Scripture" (II.1.2). In other words, since Scripture has been given as a supplement to, not a replacement for, the natural law that Hooker thinks is still more or less inscribed on our consciences, we do not always need to appeal directly to Scripture to determine the best way to act in a given circumstance. Nor do we need to fear, as Cartwright did, that our hearts cannot be assured that we are pleasing and glorifying God unless we have a scriptural prooftext for our actions. The reason which we use to judge our actions is itself God's gift to us, created for this very purpose:

> Nor let any man think that following the judgment of natural discretion in such cases we can have no assurance that we please God. For to the Author and God of our nature, how shall any operation proceeding in natural sort be in that respect unacceptable? The nature which himself hath given to work by he cannot but be delighted with, when we exercise the same any way without commandment of his to the contrary. (II.4.6)

So on closer inspection, the two issues of the *scope* of scriptural authority and the *mode* of scriptural authority are actually inseparable for Hooker. Hooker does not mean to say, as he has sometimes been read, that Scripture doesn't really tell us all that much, and outside its narrow bounds, reason is free to decide as it wishes. This is a common modern way of thinking, to be sure: over on the one side, you have your little domain of faith, where Scripture is paramount, and on the other side, you have everything else, the "secular" realm, where reason and/or individual preference reign unchallenged. This is not how Hooker sees it. On the contrary, Scripture talks about all manner of things—personal morality, politics, economic life, church discipline, and much much more. To be sure, Hooker does not want to assume, as Cartwright sometimes seems to, that Scripture must talk about absolutely everything—there are some things that really are morally indifferent in the fullest sense, among them, taking up a straw. But beyond this relatively insignificant realm, Scripture is a guide for all of life, just not in such a way as to "clean have abrogated . . . the law of nature" (II.8.6). In essentials of the faith, truths that are beyond nature, Scripture is our sole guide; in other matters, it is mediated through the prisms of reason, prudence, history, tradition, and law.

How, we may ask, can Hooker draw such a sharp line between these two? After all, even if justification is by faith alone, faith is never alone, but is always accompanied by the obedience of sanctification. How can Hooker say that Scripture is sufficient only in those few matters connected to justification? Doesn't Paul say that Scripture was given "that the man of God may be complete, equiped for every good work"? Hooker's key consideration here is *change*: "There is no reason in the world wherefore we should esteem it as necessary always to do, as always to believe, the same things; seeing every man knoweth that the matter of faith is constant, the matter contrariwise of action daily changeable" (III.10.7). In other words, it is not that Scripture does not have anything to teach us about our moral, and indeed our social and political duties, but it is that the object of this teaching is changing from day to day, unlike the unchanging truths of salvation. This does not mean that all morality is simply up for grabs, but simply that in the nature of the case, Scripture can only give us general principles and particular applications; how to apply those general principles today requires that we exercise our own prudence.

It is tempting to assume that, where Scripture *does* give us particular applications of these principles (such as in the detailed laws of the Pentateuch), here at least we have a certain rule for our actions, but Hooker points out that this is only true inasmuch as the two circumstances are the same. There are plenty of laws and exhortations in Scripture where we can still discern an enduring principle to be applied in our own day, but in which the particular application will obviously look different. (Hooker gives the example of Paul's directions to Timothy concerning the selection of widows in the church.) Often, in fact, Scripture gives us neither direct moral teaching or particular laws, but merely narration, lived examples of obedience and disobedience. Hooker notes wryly that whereas the Puritans are constantly invoking the "'the law of God,' 'the word of the Lord' . . . their common ordinary practice is to quote by-speeches in some historical narration or other, and to urge them as if they were written in most exact form of law" (III.5.1). Cartwright's appeal to Peter "standing up in the midst of the disciples," which we noted above, is a good example. Cartwright takes this description as a clear precedent to be followed, but how does he know that, really? Scripture itself doesn't tell him. In fact, there are any number of actions narrated in Scripture which are not examples to be followed. How do we know which are which? Again, Hooker says, by application of reason, experience, and our innate moral sensibilities:

> Howbeit when Scripture doth yield us precedents, how far forth they are to be followed; when it giveth natural laws, what particular order is thereunto most agreeable; when positive, which way to make laws unrepugnant unto them . . . all this must be by reason found out. And therefore, "to refuse the conduct of the light of nature," saith St. Augustine, "is not folly alone but accompanied with impiety." (III.9.1)

The result of all this, of course, is to quite invert Cartwright's dictum, that "it is the virtue of a good law to leave as little as may be in the discretion of the judge." Not that good laws should be vague for vagueness' sake, but because the nature of the world is such that no one can craft laws that apply in the same way in every circumstance, and even the divine lawmaker in Scripture does not thus ignore the nature of the world he has made; instead, he endows us with discretion to enable us to interpret and apply Scripture in our changing circumstances. Sure, this means a loss of certainty, but it was only ever a false certainty in the first place, an attempt to claim the unambiguous authority of Scripture for inherently ambiguous decisions, especially when we move beyond individual ethics to the realm of institutions and politics, Hooker's particular focus in the *Laws*. Rather than seeking in vain to resolve all uncertainties in advance, then, we must learn the art of living with uncertainty, the art of living in a culture of persuasion, by the virtue of prudence.

Nor is this a call to a postmodern relativism, for Hooker believes that human nature doesn't change all that much. His theology of law, then, is a delicate balancing act between the eternal and the temporal, and to that let us now turn our attention.

FOR DISCUSSION

1. Is the concept of "things indifferent" a useful concept? What are some different things it might mean?
2. Why were Puritans like Cartwright suspicious of the idea of "things indifferent"? How did they prefer to approach moral questions instead?
3. How does Hooker's focus on salvation as the end of Scripture transform his approach to its use in moral reasoning?
4. Do you think this is a helpful approach, or potentially problematic?

9

KEY THEMES: LAW

A LEGAL REFORMATION?

For modern theologians, especially in disestablished churches like those of the United States, *law* is rarely a central topic of discussion. To be sure, it might have a role in soteriology or redemptive history in the contrast of "Law" and "Gospel," or among Christian ethicists thinking critically about the justice or injustice of various laws (or the legitimacy of coercion altogether), but these disparate strands are rarely related to one another. More recently, we have heard a lot about "natural law," the principles of universal morality that belong to us as creatures, not merely as Christians, even from the lips of Protestant thinkers who have grown unaccustomed to the idea.

In the time of the Reformation, however, the category of law was indispensable to the theologian. It has long been common for historians to observe that the Reformation was a matter of doctrine, not of politics, and that the political changes that did occur were more a matter of opportunism than of principle. This is especially true of the Reformation in England, which many have treated as really the combination of two quite separate revolutions—the constitutional changes brought in by Henry VIII and Elizabeth, and the religious changes brought in by Protestant reformers and continued by the Puritans. But this is to ignore the fact that, on the eve of the Reformation, it was impossible to fiddle with politics without fiddling with religion, and vice versa. The pope, after all, still claimed to be the supreme power both spiritual and temporal, with authority to depose monarchs and absolve criminals. Many lesser churchmen wielded substantial political power in their hybrid offices, and civil rulers chafed at the notion of what amounted to an effectively autonomous political body—the Church—within their land: a body with its own authority structure, its own inalienable property, its own "taxes," its own system of laws and courts, and its immunity to many civil laws. In such a setting, Henry VIII's seizure of headship over the Church of England from the pope was no mere administrative reorganization, but depended upon, and entailed, dramatic shifts in the understanding of what the Church was, what the relation of clergy and laity was, and what duties God had given to rulers. Political theology was at the heart of the English Reformation, and indeed the Reformation as a whole, from the beginning.

In such a context, there was bound to be a great deal of practical wrangling and theological theorizing around the proper boundaries of civil law and ecclesiastical law, the authority that each had over the believer, and who was responsible for each. Before the Reformation, two parallel jurisdictions had arisen, constantly squabbling between one another as to the proper limits of their authority. Sometimes civil rulers gained a temporary upper hand and the support of the church authorities in their territory, but often, the pope and leading churchmen seemed to enjoy a freedom from any accountability, while themselves able to dictate the actions of civil authorities, on pain of excommunication. For most of the Reformers, then, the solution to this clash of authorities was to deprive the clergy of any claims to earthly power and make them accountable to the civil magistrates in each realm. Of course, magistrates were accountable to heed the biblical teaching of their ministers, at least insofar as it was truly faithful to Scripture, but if they disagreed with the ministers' interpretations, or simply ignored them, Protestant churchmen had little formal recourse.

Some, such as Calvin in Geneva and even more John Knox in Scotland, tried to rectify this new imbalance by putting the power of church discipline and excommunication firmly in the hands of semi-autonomous courts of ministers and elders, but others saw this as a reversion to the clashing authorities of late medieval papalism. Different communities and polities throughout the Reformation lands experimented with different ways of reconciling this tension, and most of the magisterial Reformers declared that different approaches were appropriate, depending on the political organization of a given territory and the quality of its ministers.[1] In Elizabeth's England, however, the tensions caused by her imposition of unwanted ceremonies and vestments, not to mention her refusal to reform the structure of the English episcopacy, led some Puritans to insist on the necessity of an independent system of church courts with their own ecclesiastical laws and penalties—i.e., presbyterianism.

Another new challenge for the Protestant theology of law stemmed from Luther's revolutionary understanding of faith and works: whether laws came from civil or church authorities, it was clear that the moral and soteriological

---

1. For an introductory treatment, see Ballor and Littlejohn, "European Calvinism: Church Discipline."

status of these laws had to be carefully rethought. After all, if the Christian was a "free lord of all," then was not his conscience free of all laws, even if, as "dutiful servant of all," he still obeyed them for the sake of his neighbor?[2] Certainly Luther himself in *The Freedom of a Christian*, and other Reformers after him, were adamant in insisting that justification by faith did not exempt a believer from works of love toward his neighbors, and in insisting that obedience to civil laws was a key way in which the believer showed such love. However, it would seem to follow that such laws should only be obeyed insofar as they really were, in the believer's estimation, a way of loving his neighbor. What about obviously bad laws? Was the believer obliged to obey these, even against his conscience? And if so, what became of the fundamental Protestant doctrine of the Christian's freedom of conscience? Many Reformers, when they came to speak of Romans 13 and the Christian's absolute duty to obey the magistrate, became decidedly fuzzy on the point. Others, particularly later in the sixteenth century, sought to give Christian liberty some kind of political expression by spelling out not merely the rights of rulers and duties of subjects, but the rights of subjects and duties of rulers.[3]

One way of trying to resolve this difficulty was to suggest that the magistrate should simply follow Scripture in all his law-making; that way, the subject's conscience was bound only to the authority of Scripture, not human authority per se. After all, the elevated Protestant view of Scripture, and the confidence in its relevance for all of life, had drawn theologians, especially in the emerging Reformed tradition, to sift carefully the laws of Scripture—both the civil laws of

2. These lines come from the first page of *Freedom of a Christian* (*Luther's Works*, 31:344).

3. Quentin Skinner's treatment of this development in *Foundations of Modern Political Thought*, vol. 2, chs. 7–9 remains classic.

the Old Testament and the moral laws of both testaments—for guidance for the Christian life. We have seen already how far some English Puritans took this dependence on Scripture, and its—to Hooker's mind at least—potentially disastrous consequences. For some of these Puritans, the new biblicism even entailed a return to the civil laws of the Pentateuch as the only right way of ordering a Christian society. While most of the magisterial Reformers had stopped short of drawing such implications, or even explicitly condemned them, it was an easy temptation to succumb to in an age filled with heady enthusiasm about the renewing power of the Word of God, and its superiority to all human authority.

THE REFORMED THOMIST REVIVAL

By the late sixteenth century, then, there was a widely-felt need for comprehensive and coherent Reformed theology of law. One obvious place to look for such an account was in the medieval scholasticism of Thomas Aquinas and many of his contemporaries and successors. After all, whatever things the later Middle Ages had lacked, systematic completeness and coherence was not among them. In Aquinas's influential formulation, all law could be understood as a participation in, or an echo of, the one *eternal law* that guides all things to their proper end.[4] This eternal law is none other than a reflection of the nature of God himself, which although free is not arbitrary, but rational and regular, establishing the blueprint according to which he has created and governs all else. As mediated to creation, then,

---

4. *Summa theologiae* IaIIae Q. 93. In Dyson, ed., *Aquinas: Political Writings*, 101. Aquinas's full discussion of law may be found in *Summa* IaIIae Qs. 90–108; Qs. 90–97 are found in Dyson, 76–157. Perhaps the best recent exposition of Aquinas's theory of natural law can be found in Porter, *Nature as Reason*.

and inscribed in every creature, especially humankind, this law becomes the *natural law*, which directs each creature to the goal God has made it for, warning it against any irrational actions that might bring lasting harm. For humans, this natural law is discerned not only by instinct, but also by reason, and hence becomes the object of careful moral deliberation and application. To provide some order to this process of deliberation and application, since people are liable to disagree and have clashing interests, *human law* is necessary, in which political authorities, deliberating on the needs of the common good, in accordance with the *natural law*, make binding determinations to guide the actions of their communities.

Finally, for Aquinas, there is the *divine law* (Scripture), divided into the *old law* (Old Testament) and *new law* (New Testament). This is necessary for four reasons: (1) to direct man to eternal happiness, rather than mere earthly happiness; (2) to resolve disagreements in the understanding and application of the natural law; (3) to regulate attitudes of the heart which lie beyond the reach of human law; (4) to comprehensively address all sinful acts, which human law cannot do. It is worth noting that, in this explanation, Aquinas really distinguishes between two very different kinds or functions of divine law: with respect to the first reason, divine law is of a wholly different order than natural law, taking us quite beyond it to a supernatural end; with respect to the latter three reasons, divine law stands in parallel to human law, applying and specifying the natural law for the sake of good living (only more clearly and comprehensively than human law could do).

It makes sense, then, that after the initial dust of the Reformation had settled, Protestant theologians began to adapt Aquinas's theology of law into a Protestant theological framework.[5] In 1576 the Heidelberg theologian Jerome Zanchi, a student and friend of Peter Martyr Vermigli, attempted this in his treatise *De Lege in Genere* (*On the Law in General*), though it remained unpublished until 1597.[6] In 1592 Franciscus Junius, the newly-appointed professor of theology at Leiden University, responded to a request from the city magistrates with a treatise *De Politiae Mosis Observatione* (*On the Observation of the Mosaic Polity*), which sought to address how far, if at all, the Mosaic civil laws bound Reformed magistrates in his own day.[7] Beginning with a systematic account of the different classes of law, he shows that, as divinely-authorized *human laws* (i.e., fulfilling the second of Aquinas's four purposes), these laws were made to govern the specific needs of the Israelite people in that time and place, and do not directly bind other peoples in other times and places. Both Junius and Zanchi construct their classifications of law in clear imitation of Aquinas, though with the noteworthy difference that, as Reformed theologians, they do not make such a separation between the Old and New Testaments, treating them together as one divine law. A few years later, the eminent Protestant jurist Johannes Althusius, who is still extensively studied by political theorists today, drew upon the work of Zanchi and Junius, together with his own exhaustive knowledge of classical and medieval sources, to construct a

---

5. It should be noted that in this, as in most other achievements the Reformed are noted for, the Lutherans had preceded them. See for instance the discussion of Johann Oldendorp in Witte, *Law and Reformation*, ch. 4, and of Niels Hemmingsen in Hutchinson and Maas, "Niels Hemmingsen and the Development of Lutheran Natural-Law Teaching."

6. This was published in translation by Jeffrey J. Veenstra, *On the Law in General* (2012).

7. This was published in a translation by Todd Rester, *The Mosaic Polity* (2015).

Reformed theory of politics, the *Politica* (1603), and of law, the *Dicaeologica* (1618).[8]

So we should not be surprised to find that Richard Hooker, taking up his pen around the year 1590 to defend the ecclesiastical laws of England, draws similarly upon the received Thomistic categories, seeking to flesh them out into a comprehensive theory that will make sense of the roles of rulers and subjects, kings and priests, Scripture and reason. In fact, although many Hooker scholars have made much of his dependence on Aquinas, he actually tweaks the Thomistic schema more than either Zanchi or Junius.[9] Of course, there is no space here to go into a close comparison of these four expositions, though I will note some of Hooker's tweaks in passing, as I briefly sketch how Hooker defines the major categories of law. I will also note how this classification helps him, like Junius, resolve the problem of the place of the Mosaic civil law. It also informs his discussion of the relation of civil and ecclesiastical law, though we will postpone discussion of this to the next chapter, on his ecclesiology. What I will say a bit more about here, however, is how Hooker tackles the thorniest problem above: the liberty of conscience in relation to law, and the limitations on the law-making power of rulers.

HOOKER'S CLASSIFICATION OF LAW

When we think about the different contexts within which we use the word "law," it might seem at first glance that they have little in common: the law of gravity, the law of

8. The standard translation of the the *Politica* is that of Carney (1964); a portion of *Dicaeologica* has been published in translation by Jeffrey J. Veenstra as *On Law and Power* (2013).

9. For a very fine treatment of "Thomism" in the sixteenth century and Hooker's relationship to it, see Paul Dominiak's forthcoming "Hooker, Scholasticism, and Reformed Orthodoxy."

non-contradiction, tax laws, the moral law, the law of charity, etc. Perhaps "law" is just one of those English words with several different meanings. Hooker, however, is eager to demonstrate that all of the many different laws which he discusses in his *Laws* are really all forms of the same basic kind of thing: "A law therefore generally taken is a directive rule unto goodness of operation," he summarizes at one point (I.8.4). This definition highlights his Aristotelian emphasis on teleology: everything has a purpose; that which helps it attain the purpose is good for it, and that which hinders it is bad; law, then, is that which directs every particular thing toward its good end. He elaborates at the very beginning of the *Laws*:

> All things that are have some operation not violent or casual. Neither doth any thing ever begin to exercise the same without some foreconceived end for which it worketh. And the end which it worketh for is not obtained, unlesse the worke be also fit to obtain it by. For unto every end every operation will not serve. That which doth appoint the form and measure of working, the same we term a *Law*. (I.2.1)

This is how he can speak of God himself as law-bound, since all God's works are ordered, rational, and directed to his glory and the good of his creatures. Not that there is some law outside of God that governs his being; rather, his being *is* this law, a law that encompasses every kind of law, inasmuch as God's operations encompass all that is; it is "that order which God before all ages hath set down with himself, for himself to do all things by" (I.2.6). Now, interestingly, here Hooker departs from Aquinas in distinguishing between the "first law eternal" which governs God's own secret will, and the "second law eternal" as "that which with himself he hath set down as expedient to be kept by all his creatures" (I.3.1).

The reason for this distinction (which mirrors one implicit in Hooker's contemporary Junius) appears to be Hooker's concern to void blurring the distinction between Creator and creature, as if we could simply reason our way up from the natural law—what we rationally ought to do—to that which God rationally ought to do.[10]

In any case, though, the second eternal law is, like Aquinas's eternal law, the archetypal form from which all the other forms of law derive:

> That part of it which ordereth natural agents, we call usually *nature's* law: that which Angels do clearly behold, and without any swerving observe, is a law *celestial* and heavenly; the law of *reason* that which bindeth creatures reasonable in the world, and with which by reason they may most plainly perceive themselves bound; that which bindeth them, and is not known but by special revelation from God, *Divine* law; *human* law that which out of the law either of reason or of God, men probably gathering to be expedient, they make it a law. (I.3.1)

We can see here two more tweaks to Aquinas's taxonomy, though neither is particularly important. For one, Thomas never speaks of "celestial law" which governs angels, even though he certainly has plenty to say about the nature of angels in the *Summa*, so it's not surprising that Hooker should add the category. Also, although Thomas distinguishes between between the way irrational creatures and rational humans grasp the natural law, he still treats these under the same heading, whereas Hooker puts them under two different headings, "nature's law" and "law of reason" (although he will sometimes refer to both simply

---

10. See further my forthcoming essay, "Hooker, Junius, and a Reformed Theology of Law."

as "natural law," so there is little practical difference). Just as "nature's law" guides irrational creatures to their appointed end and perfection, their unique form of participation in divine goodness, so does the law of reason guide mankind, only that we are uniquely called to reflect on, discern, and actively pursue the goodness proper to our natures, which uniquely image the divine nature. Man thus seeks not only after the perfections proper to all creatures, but to further perfections: "such as are not for any other cause, then for knowledge itself desired ... [through which] by proceeding in the knowledge of truth and by growing in the exercise of virtue, man amongst the creatures of this inferior world, aspireth to the greatest conformity with God" (I.5.3).

By recognizing those goods which constitute the perfection of our nature and gaining experience in pursuing them, we derive maxims and axioms as a guide to right conduct. Of course, these are not always easy to discern, since there are a multitude of possible goods to choose from, and we often choose a less over a greater, or a faulty route to a genuine good. Nevertheless, "there is not that good which concerneth us, but it hath evidence enough for itself, if reason were diligent to search it out" (I.7.7). Reason can thus grasp some basic human duties toward God, and also the general principles of what we owe to our neighbors. Of course, as we have already seen, Hooker is not at all blind to the effect of sin, which frequently interferes with our ability to reason toward the good (not to mention our willingness to act on this knowledge!), and leaves us in need of the help of divine law.

Before treating of "the divine law," though, Hooker, like Aquinas, discusses human law, as the chief means by which the general principles of the law of reason are rendered concrete. Human law is more than mere rational deliberation about what the law of reason requires in relation to a concrete problem; deliberation can do no more than provide maxims of prudent action for private individuals. Human law has a necessarily *political* dimension; it is law promulgated and in some sense enforced for a community of men and women bound together by compact, by representatives authorized to act on behalf of the whole. (We will say a bit more about the implications of this theory of representation below.) Following Aquinas, though with his own terminology, Hooker distinguishes between what he calls "mixedly" and "merely" human laws. The former are those which simply reassert what reason could probably have already told us, and add rewards and punishments to motivate us (for instance, laws against murder). The latter are those which, although in harmony with the law of reason, go beyond it, specifying things in a way that is just, but which does not exclude other approaches as necessarily unjust (for instance, laws governing inheritance, which have differed dramatically through the centuries). Within this section, Hooker draws attention to a fact that is central to his argument throughout the *Laws*: the vast diversity, and constant mutability, of human societies and circumstances, means that "one kind of laws cannot serve for all kinds of regiment" (I.10.9): laws have to be particularly fitted to their time place.

Finally, then, Hooker comes to divine law (Scripture), and in his exposition he draws a clear distinction between the two very different kinds of divine law, which we noted above was merely implicit in Aquinas. He treats of the first—laws that are supernatural "both in respect of the manner of delivering them which is divine" (supernatural in origin), "and also in regard of the the things delivered which are such as . . . God ordained besides the course of nature to rectify nature's obliquity" (supernatural in object)—in chapter 11 of Book I of the *Laws*. Only then does he, in chapter 12, discuss laws that are supernatural in origin, but natural in object—divinely-authorized restatements or specifications of natural and human law. This distinction becomes critical to Hooker's argument in the rest of the *Laws*, for it makes clear that one cannot simply say, "the Bible says so," and apply all parts of Scripture in the same way. We saw this in the previous chapter: only when it comes to man's supernatural end, for which Scripture is indeed alone necessary and sufficient, does divine law necessarily bind us always in the same way. The requirement to "believe that Jesus is Christ the Son of God" will never change. But what about when Scripture is restating duties that belong to us simply as created human beings? Well, the general principles of these duties do not change, and indeed, these too are in their own way necessary to salvation: "Love the Lord your God with all your heart, and all your soul, and all your mind, and your neighbor as yourself." But the concrete application of such moral duties to the vicissitudes of human life, particularly to the complexities of social and political life, *do* change, so that when it comes to these aspects of Scripture, divine law has the same basic status as human law (only more trustworthy).

This leads Hooker to the same conclusion as his contemporary Junius regarding the status of the Mosaic laws: just because they were God-given for the ancient Israelites does not make them perpetually binding on us. Not only are some of them abrogated because their *end* was temporary, like the ceremonial laws fulfilled in the work of Christ, but even others for which the end remains (i.e., restraining violent acts), may change if the circumstances and societies they are governing change. When his opponents complain that it is "execrable pride and presumption" for humans to change laws instituted by God, Hooker responds with a sentence that might almost serve as a motto for his whole theory of law: "Wherein they mark not that laws are instruments to rule by, and that instruments are not only to be framed according unto the general end for which they are provided, but even according unto that very particular, which riseth out of the matter whereon they have to work" (III.10.3). In other words, just as a carpenter may need many tools to accomplish the same task (nails and hammers, screws and screwdrivers, bolts and wrenches), depending on the type and shape of wood he is dealing with, so it is with human laws. Therefore even laws given by God himself may be changed inasmuch as the "matter whereon they have to work" has changed.

Hooker will contend that this is just as true of ecclesiastical laws as of civil laws, but to follow this argument, we will first have to look at his theology of the church, which must wait till the next chapter.

LAW, LIBERTY, AND CONSCIENCE

What, then, of law's relation to conscience? After all, we noted that for Luther and the other Reformers, no human authority could bind the conscience, strictly speaking, and yet Hooker has carved out a wide scope for human authority in lawmaking. Does this mean that Hooker, like many of his conformist predecesssors, has no answer for Puritan objectors besides, "It's the law. Yours not to reason why, yours but to shut up and obey"?[11] Hooker, after all, had declared at the outset of the *Laws* that "my whole endeavor is to resolve the conscience, and to show as near as I can what in this controversy the heart is to think" (Pref. 7.1). Over and over he declares that the root of the Puritan and

---

11. This is only slightly a caricature, as one can see from consulting Richard Bancroft's *Sermon Preached at Pauls Crosse* (1588). See further my essay, "Bancroft *versus* Penry."

presbyterian protest is a failure to understand the different kinds of law, the rationales behind the laws that are currently established, and how these laws are conducive to the good of the church and the realm (or at the very least, are not harmful to it). If his opponents but follow his argument, he suggests, their cheerful obedience will follow as a matter of course. From this standpoint, it is not the laws as such that bind the conscience; rather, their intrinsic rationality elicits the morally-attuned conscience's free assent. This all sounds very wonderful, but what about when it doesn't work this way? What if subjects simply fail to see how the laws in question are rational, and feel compelled to disobey? Worse still, what if the dissenters are right, and the laws in question *are* irrational and unjust?

These questions sit right at the heart of the whole tradition of Christian political thought, with its foundational declaration that "we must obey God rather than man" (Acts 5:29), so there is no way we can tackle them comprehensively here.[12] And I should add that Hooker's own full solution to the problem is not clear: the one part of the *Laws* where he tackles the question head-on, in Book VIII, chapter 6, remains tantalizingly unfinished. In fact, after saying that some err by minimizing disobedience to human laws, and others by making every breach of human law to be sin against God, it concludes with the maddening declaration: "A mean there is between these extremities, if so be we can find it out" (VIII.6.9).[13] But if Hooker ever found it

12. For those interested in pursuing them further, see my forthcoming book, *The Freedom of a Christian Commonwealth*.

13. Note that this section does not appear within the body of the *Laws* in Keble's nineteenth-century edition, since he deemed it an extraneous fragment that had mistakenly gotten attached to Book VIII. It appears instead as "Appendix No. I., *Supposed Fragment of a Sermon on Civil Obedience, hitherto printed as part of the Eighth Book.*" This citation is valid, however, for both the Folger and McGrade editions.

out, we, alas, cannot find it out from him. However, he gives us enough to go on in the *Laws* to reconstruct key aspects of his attitude toward conscience, liberty, and human law.

The first thing to note is that while for Hooker, conscience clearly consists in the exercise of our reason to discern the voice of God, reasoning is rarely a purely individual undertaking. On the contrary, our consciences are formed from childhood in a milieu of traditional teachings and customs, receiving the wisdom of our parents and ancestors, and this dependency is only reduced, not done away with, when we reach adulthood. Particularly when it comes to reasoning about laws that affect the entire commonwealth, "men of common capacity and but ordinary judgment are not able (for how should they?) to discern what things are fittest for each kind and state of regiment" (I.10.7). In such matters, it is only rational for individual reason to defer to the judgments of the wisest in the realm, which are generally reflected, he optimistically deemed, in its laws. Such deference is an *exercise* of our freedom, not a loss of it; on the contrary, to defiantly act on our own ill-informed preferences would be to fall back into the bondage of ignorance. In Hooker's thought, then, government should be understood as a *corporate exercise of reason*, in which the less educated and less wise participate by deferring to the judgment of the more educated and more wise. No doubt in our much more democratic age, many will balk at such elitism, and yet Hooker might well respond by pointing out that every government, whether we like it or not, depends upon an elite—the only question is whether that elite will be defined by birth and marriage, by wealth, or by wisdom.[14] To be sure, Hooker was no doubt

14. In contemporary "democratic" America, for instance, it is clear to most any impartial observer that the first two factors are the actually decisive ones. As this book is being drafted, the leading candidates for the 2016 presidency are the brother and son of a recent president (Jeb Bush) and the wife of another (Hillary Clinton).

aware that the first two factors were in fact the decisive ones in English politics of his day, but he at least tried to sketch his "rule of the wisest" as a hopeful political vision, which would come to some brief fruition in the England of James I.

The second part of Hooker's approach is his vision of government as a *corporate exercise of will*, an idea that modern Americans in particular have strangely lost. Even in a political system where Parliament was only just beginning to develop into its role of providing representation and signifying the consent of the governed, Hooker could declare that *consent* was fundamental to the concept of law, and no ruler could hold legitimate authority without at least the implicit consent of the governed (VIII.3.2). This consent does not come via a referendum on every political question, but through the fact that we are able to act through others as our representatives: "Although we be not personally our selves present, notwithstanding our assent is by reason of others, agents there in our behalf. And what we do by others, no reason but that it should stand as our deed, no less effectually to bind us then if ourselves had done it in person" (I.10.8). In other words, we can bind ourselves by the actions of our representatives: "A law is the deed of the whole body politic, whereof if ye judge yourselves to be any part, then is the law even your deed also" (Pref. 5.2). This statement, though it comes at the beginning of the *Laws*, could be considered the capstone of Hooker's argument. Indeed, in it he portrays the political citizen as mirroring the logic of God's own action—remaining free even in being bound by law, because this law is his own rational action. What this means is that even when we do not necessarily agree with the laws our representatives have made, we accept them as actions taken on our behalf, until such time as, by respectful petition, we may have those laws changed.

Of course, this does not resolve the question of what we ought to do if our representatives act as tyrants, or pass laws so clearly unjust that we must personally disclaim them and disobey them. Hooker neatly sidesteps the question of active resistance to unjust rulers, even if some of his successors, like John Locke, were to develop his ideas in this direction. And this is perhaps fair enough, given his purposes. After all, a key part of his argument is to show that the questions at issue in the debate over English ecclesiastical laws are by definition *adiaphora*, "things indifferent." Not in the sense that they don't matter at all, but that they are the sort of things that by their nature may vary by time and place, and must be judged by the probable reason of prudence, rather than by the necessary reason of logical demonstration, or direct divine revelation. Accordingly, he grants that, on any matter in which a dissenting subject has a *necessary* argument against the rightness of the laws, such an argument "dischargeth . . . the conscience, and setteth it at full liberty." But if the argument is merely *probable*, as Hooker thinks it must be in the present case, then, "of peace and quietness there is not any way possible, unless the probable voice of every entire society or body politic overrule all private of like nature in the same body" (Pref. 6.6). Unless the probable reasoning of public authorities, acting in our name, can trump our own disagreements based on probable reasoning, then there will be no basis for law and order, and every man will do what is right in his own eyes. No doubt Hooker's stance looks worrisomely authoritarian from our twenty-first-century perspective, but if anything it seemed the opposite in the sixteenth century, and he did, after all, have a point: injustice, even on a large scale, can rarely do as much harm as quickly as anarchy can.

FOR DISCUSSION

1. What are some reasons why *law* was an important theme for the Protestant Reformers?

2. What are Hooker's four main categories of law and how do they relate to one another? What is the value of these distinctions?

3. Do you find Hooker's concept of government as a "corporate exercise of reason" and a "corporate exercise of will" persuasive and helpful? Why or why not?

10

KEY THEMES: CHURCH

THE QUEST FOR THE TRUE CHURCH

WHAT IS "THE CHURCH"? Where is the "true church" to be found? Many modern Christians go their whole lives without losing sleep over such questions, but few questions were so central to the sixteenth-century Reformation as these. For centuries Western Christians, whatever their uncertainties about their own personal salvation, at least had no doubt whether the community of salvation, the body of Christ, was to be found. It was visible—indeed, all too visible in the wealth and power of the papal hierarchy. All the Catholic faithful were in some sense the church, but the unity and visibility of the church was guaranteed above all by the clergy, with the pope at their head, who, whatever their personal faults, could reliably represent Christ to believers. But what if they couldn't? What if the monks, the clergy, the pope himself could become enemies unto the gospel? Where then was the church to be found? And if the rites of the church were not the channels of grace, outside of which there was no salvation, should they then be cast aside as needless or even stumbling blocks to faith?

These were the questions that vexed the magisterial Reformers and their heirs, faced on one side with an unrelenting tide of Catholic polemic that could point, if not to a pure body of Christ, at least to a unified one, and on the other side with sects of radical Protestants who demanded a fully pure and holy church, even at the cost of unity.

If the Catholic church had become so corrupt as to warrant separation, then, some of Luther's followers asked, was this separated, pure community of believers the true church? The Anabaptists, arising within a few years of the beginning of the Reformation, certainly thought so. But Luther himself recognized that such a position endangered the all-important affirmation of justification by faith—faith, after all, was in itself invisible, and such attempts to define the church around a visible community of pure saints had to lay too much stress on works. Luther's concept of the justified sinner, *simul justus et peccator*, therefore provided something of a framework for his ecclesiology. The church was on one level perfectly righteous by virtue of its union with Christ, but this union, and this righteous identity, were hidden; as manifest in the world, in history, it was still sinful and failing, a *corpus permixtum* composed of wheat and tares, gradually being sanctified. And yet given the proliferation of sects in the early Reformation, and pressure from Catholic apologists to prove that their church was not simply a "Platonic form," the Reformers began to develop certain "notes" or "marks" by which the true church could be visibly recognized. The Augsburg Confession of 1530 established two marks: "The Church is the congregation of saints, in which the Gospel is rightly taught and the Sacraments are rightly administered," but some over the next couple decades, wanting to emphasize that just as true Christians must be characterized by godly life, so must the true church, added a third, "discipline," which initially had quite a broad sense, rather than simply designating excommunication and its precursors.[1]

Now, these were all fairly useful in giving you a decent idea of where the church *was* (although they obviously could not stand alone; they presupposed a Protestant understanding of what the Gospel and sacraments were): if you saw a minister faithfully expounding the text of Scripture, and administering baptism and the Lord's Supper, well then you could assume that there was a manifestation of Christ's body—imperfect, perhaps, but in communion with the Head. But they weren't so good at telling you where the church *wasn't*.[2] How false did a church's preaching have to be before it could no longer count as part of the body of Christ? How distorted or rationalistic or superstitious did its sacramental practice have to be? How lax did its discipline have to be? In response to Catholic polemic and persecution, many Protestants in the latter half of the sixteenth century, particularly among the Reformed, increasingly deployed the *notae ecclesiae* to brand Rome as a wholly false church, and in the process, felt the need to lay increasing stress on the adverb *"rightly."* Some also tended to redefine "discipline" specifically in terms of a structure of church government, namely Presbyterianism, without which, it was suggested, a minister could not *rightly* preach or administer the sacraments.

Such a sharp blade of division, wielded zealously, could quickly be turned upon other Protestants, as it was in Elizabethan England. There, militant presbyterians suggested

[1]. See P. D. L. Avis, "'The True Church' in Reformation Theology," 319–45; Ballor and Littlejohn, "Ecclesiastical Discipline."

[2]. Avis, "True Church," 334: "The *notae ecclesiae* is a qualitative concept; theoretically one can say whether a certain ecclesial body possesses the marks or not. But in practice it was found to need supplementing by a quantitative one, such as Calvin's concept that Rome contained the *vestigia* of the church."

that the Church of England was not in fact a true church, despite its Protestant confession, due to the deficiencies in its preaching, sacraments, and discipline.[3] Although most equivocated and held back from quite following through on the implications of this charge, others did not, and broke away into separatism. The separatists, in turn, by application of the same principles, tended to divide and divide still further, especially after their emigration to America. This was clearly not a sustainable path, and in any case, it ran the very risk that Luther had earlier perceived in Anabaptism. We saw in previous chapters that many Puritans in Hooker's day were quite preoccupied with the assurance of their salvation, and with assurance that they were following God's Word to the T. To provide such assurance, some at least tended to move further away from simple faith and to rely more and more on concrete indicators. The same process was at work in the attempt to know for sure what wasn't a faithful church and what was, and when one was in it. The risk of Pharisaism in such a context was real.

At the same time, most English conformists found themselves defending a fairly elaborate structure of sacraments, liturgy, fasts and feasts that they were not altogether comfortable with. Inheriting the Reformers' suspicions about the role of such outward forms in communicating grace, many of them, such as Archbishop John Whitgift, laid much more stress on the fact that the forms were commanded by law—"they were there because they were there," in the words of Peter Lake[4]—than that they were integral to the church's spiritual life. No wonder many puritans, seeking a purer church but unwilling to separate, were frustrated!

Richard Hooker's delicately balanced ecclesiology must be understood against this complex backdrop. The balance

3. Avis, "True Church," 337–39.
4. Lake, *Anglicans and Puritans*, 164.

which I speak of here is of course the balance between the categories of the "visible" and "invisible" church, which had dominated Protestant ecclesiology since Luther. These terms did not simply distinguish between the pure, invisible body of the elect, and the mixed visible body of saints and hypocrites as it appears on earth; they distinguished also between the two planes on which even true believers experienced their union with Christ. On the one hand they rested entirely on Christ alone, completely righteous in him, though not in themselves; on the other hand they rested upon the visible community of saints and the outward means God had ordained to inspire and nourish their faith and love. Hooker, like many Protestant scholastics of his time, insisted on the importance of precisely and rigorously distinguishing even in things that are inseparably united; accordingly, we find in his theology both a careful affirmation of the profound difference between the church as visible and as invisible, between the inward and outward means of grace, and at the same time a clear stress on the unity of these two realms in the lives of the saints. Likewise, Hooker balances a striking minimalism when it comes to what counts as a church, with a surprising maximalism when it comes to the ways in which the church is made to participate in the life of heaven.

Unfortunately, many Hooker scholars have been unwilling to follow Hooker's own precision and balance, instead collapsing the two sides of this dialectic into a fuzzy synthesis that can mean, well, whatever anyone wants it to. In this chapter, accordingly, I will dedicate my attention primarily to the stark distinctions that Hooker draws between the church as we experience it on earth and the church as mystically united to Christ. In the next chapter, we will, as it were, put Humpty-Dumpty back together again, by showing how, according to Hooker, we nevertheless participate in the invisible grace of God by the visible signs that make up the corporate life of the church. So first, the distinctions.

"REMOVED ALTOGETHER FROM SENSE"

It is perhaps among the more curious phenomena of Hooker scholarship that, whatever their other disagreements, most Hooker scholars can at least agree that Hooker has little interest, unlike his Protestant predecessors, in distinguishing the visible and invisible churches; instead, he intends to "conflate" the two, so that "the invisible church essentially becomes one with the visible."[5] I hate to set myself against such a strong consensus, but there is simply no textual evidence for this claim. At the outset of a chapter of the *Laws* entitled, "What the Church is, and in what respect Laws of Polity are thereunto necessarily required," Hooker begins instead with quite a rigorous assertion of classic distinction:

> That Church of Christ which we properly term his body mystical, can be but one, neither can that one be sensibly discerned by any man . . . Only our minds by intellectual conceit [conception] are able to apprehend, that such a real body there is . . . a body mystical, because the mystery of their conjunction is removed altogether from sense. (III.1.2)

The visible church, on the other hand, is a "sensibly known company," identified by the "outward profession of those thinges, which supernaturally appertain to the very essence of Christianity, and are necessarily required in every particular Christian man" (III.1.3, 4). Hooker is quite

---

5. Lake, *Anglicans and Puritans*, 180; Harrison, "The Church," 312. See further Harrison, 306–12; Haugaard, introduction, 172–73; Neelands, "Identity of the Visible and Invisible Church," 109.

consistent in this kind of language, frequently employing "mystical" and "visible" as opposites in this context.[6]

Of course, Hooker's use of the term "mystical," rather than "invisible," has been highlighted by scholars who want to read Hooker as collapsing or obscuring the traditional distinction.[7] "Mystical" after all, has sacramental overtones, and sounds like "mysterious," which is vague enough to suggest somehow some kind of third plane that is neither quite visible or invisible. But in the sixteenth century, at least, "mystical" often seems to be little more than a synonym for "invisible," and Hooker's usage gives us no reason to go beyond this gloss. After all, his definition here—unable to "be sensibly discerned by any man," "removed altogether from sense"—sounds a lot like "invisible." And at the end of Book III he makes the equation explicit: "so far forth as the Church is the mystical body of Christ and his invisible spouse, it needeth no external polity. That very part of the law divine which teacheth faith and works of righteousness is itself alone sufficient for the Church of God in that respect. But as the Church is a visible society and body politic, laws of polity it cannot want" (III.11.14).[8] (We will shortly come back to Hooker's important point here about "laws of polity.") In short, there is no reason to assume, at least in Hooker's foundational exposition in III.1 of the *Laws*, that he intends to blur in any way what had become

---

6. See also, for instance, *First Sermon on Jude*, in *FLE* 5:13; *Laws* III.1.2, 3, 8, 9, 13, 14. The only exception to this usage is in V.24.1—"we are joined as parts to that visible mystical body which is his Church."

7. See for instance Haugaard, introduction, 172–73; Harrison, 306; Avis, *Anglicanism and the Christian Church*, 34.

8. For another equation of "mystical" and "invisible" see V.67.11, in which Hooker calls the sacraments "such instruments as mystically yet truly, invisibly yet really work our communion or fellowship with the person of Jesus Christ."

the standard Protestant distinction between the church visible and invisible. On the contrary, it seems evident that he intends, if anything, to distinguish them *more* rigorously, abandoning the whole *notae* approach to ecclesiology of his predecessors, which had led some Puritans to attempt to define the limits of the *true* visible church in such a way as to exclude all the unregenerate.[9]

Hooker consistently eschews any such attempt to police the boundaries of the church by reading others' hearts. "We cannot examine the hearts of other men, we may our own,"[10] he says in his *First Sermon Upon Part of S. Jude*, the earliest of his extant works. He explains further:

> Who be inwardly in heart the lively members of this body, and the polished stones of this building, coupled and joined to Christ, as *flesh of his flesh and bones of his bones* by the mutual bond of his unspeakable love towards them, and their unfeigned faith in him, thus linked and fastened each to other by a spiritual, sincere, and hearty affection of love without any manner of simulation, who be Jews within, and what their names be, none can tell, save he whose eyes do behold the secret disposition of all men's hearts. We, whose eyes are too dim to behold the inward man, must leave the secret judgment of every servant to his own Lord, accounting and using all men as brethren both near and dear unto us, supposing Christ to love them tenderly, so as they keep the profession of the Gospel and join in the outward communion of saints.[11]

---

9. See Avis, "True Church," 341–43.
10. *FLE* 5:28.
11. FLE 5:25–26.

Key Themes: Church

When it comes to the church in its invisible identity, hidden in Christ with God, the Lord knows those who are his, and we do not. Sure, we can make some pretty decent guesses based on outward behavior, but in the end, only God knows the heart. There is simply nothing to be gained, Hooker contends, from going around trying to determine with any level of certainty who is genuinely invisibly united to Christ and who is not. To be sure, he notes that someone may break the profession of the gospel (by heresy), to forsake the communion of saints (by schism), or to abandon all pretense of faith (by apostasy), and that in that case, "it is no injury to term them as they are,"[12] as those who have truly separated themselves from the body.

By the time he writes the *Laws*, however, he is even more wary of the attempt to identify unsound members of the body, insisting that we must "observ[e] the difference, first between the Church of God mystical and visible, then between the visible sound and corrupted" (*Laws* III.1.9). In other words, even the blatantly corrupt elements of the visible church (which included, for him, the church of Rome) still qualified as part of the visible church.

> If by external profession they be Christians, then are they of the visible Church of Christ: and Christians by external profession they are all, whose mark of recognizance hath in it those things which we have mentioned, yea, although they be impious idolaters, wicked heretics, persons excommunicable, yea, and cast out for notorious improbity. Such withal we deny not to be the imps and limbs of Satan, even as long as they continue such. (III.1.7)

In other words, of his three categories from the sermon on Jude, now only apostasy actually cuts one off from

---

12. *FLE* 5:26.

the visible church altogether. Short of that point, those who have received baptism, and still *profess* faith in Christ, should be numbered as members of the visible body, even if, to all visible appearances, they are members of the mystical body of Satan, not of Christ.

This conviction has quite practical consequences for Hooker's theory of church discipline; while he accepts excommunication as a useful tool of pastoral rebuke, he does not consider it to actually have the effect of cutting someone off from the visible church.[13] Moreover, he does not agree with the Puritan program of meticulously examining all would-be communicants to see if their faith is genuine or if they are closet papists. Accordingly, the fullest defense of his minimalist ecclesiology comes in the section of the *Laws* where he defends the eucharistic practice of the Church of England. There he insists that:

> But of the Visible Church of Christ in this present world, from which they separate all papists, we are thus persuaded: *Church* is a word which art hath devised thereby to sever and distinguish that society of men which professeth the true religion from the rest which profess it not. . . . He that will teach what *the Church* is shall never rightly perform the work whereabout he goeth, till *in matter of religion* he touch that difference which severeth the Church's Religion from theirs who are not the Church. . . . We must define the Church which is a religious society by such differences as do properly explain the essence of such things, that is to say, by the object or matter whereabout the contemplations and actions of the Church are properly conversant. . . . The *only object* which separateth ours from other religions is Jesus Christ. (V.68.6)

13. See further my essay, "Use and Abuse of John Jewel."

Therefore, he concludes, only profession of faith in Jesus Christ is necessary to count one as a member of the visible church, just as only true faith in Jesus Christ is necessary to make one a member of the invisible.

THE CHURCH AS A BODY POLITIC

Perhaps the most important effect of this minimalist ecclesiology, this sharp distinction between visible and invisible, is to open up space for Hooker's understanding of the laws of church polity. As we noted in the last chapter, when Hooker gives his taxonomy of laws, he classifies ecclesiastical laws right alongside civil laws as a form of human positive law, applied from the law of reason to the needs of concrete circumstances, and changeable as those circumstances change. This ought not surprise us in light of the fact that Hooker describes the church, as we just saw above, as a "visible society and a body politic"; as such, it needs laws just as much as any other body politic. But how does Hooker arrive at this notion?

A key part of his argument, as Torrance Kirby has shown, is to follow Luther in using the framework of justification and sanctification to talk about the two dimensions of the church. He describes the mystical church in terms of the passivity of justification, which freely receives and rests on the promises of God by faith, and the visible church with the activity of sanctification, which responds to grace, seeking to become more like Christ: "And as those everlasting promises of love, mercy, and blessednes belong to the mystical Church; even so on the other side when we reade of any duty which the Church of God is bound unto, the Church whom this doth concern is a sensibly known company" (III.1.3). The former is *justus*, pure and righteous in the sight of God (III.1.2), the latter is *peccator*, a mixed company in which are many who are the very "imps and limbs of Satan" (III.1.7). Accordingly, as Hooker later explains when outlining his theology of worship, the outward visible church should be always striving toward a fuller correspondence with the inward mystical church: "That which inwardly each man should be, the Church outwardly ought to testify" (V.6.2). Moreover, to these two kingdoms correspond, as for Luther, two *regiments*, two different ways in which these two dimensions of the church are ruled: one in which Christ alone works "secretly, inwardly, and invisibly" as "that fountain, from whence the influence of heavenly grace distilleth," and the other "external and visible in the Church, exercised by men" (VIII.4.9). Laws of church polity are those which govern the latter (III.1.14).

The outward, visible church, engaged in the process of sanctification, is Hooker's primary concern in the *Laws*,[14] and Hooker is keen to oppose the presbyterian tendency to spiritualize this visible church, thus attributing the perfection of the mystical church, *justus* in Christ, to the visible, still very much *peccator*. The result, as Kirby notes, "is a 'humanizing' of the church as an external, political organization, with the consequence that there is no longer a theological or metaphysical necessity for an 'essential' distinction to be drawn between ecclesiastical and civil power; both belong properly to the sphere of the 'politique societie.'"[15] Hooker accordingly proceeds in the remainder of Book III to explain why church polity, as an external government of the visible church that does not belong to the realm of faith and salvation, is mutable like any other earthly government:

> There is no reason in the world wherefore we should esteem it as necessary always to do, as

---

14. See Harrison, "Powers of Nature and Influences of Grace," 15–18.

15. "From 'Generall Meditations' to 'Particular Decisions,'" 62.

> always to believe the same things; seeing every man knoweth that the matter of faith is constant, the matter contrariwise of action daily changeable, especially the matter of action belonging unto Church polity.... Which kind of laws (for as much as they are not in themselves necessary to salvation) may after they are made be also changed as the difference of times or places shall require" (III.10.7).

Hooker has thus provided a theological foundation for his claim that the church, as a "politic society," functions within the sphere of human law. Therefore, to say that Scripture does not strictly bind us on these matters is in no way to demean or dismiss Scripture, but simply to understand that Scripture necessarily functions differently as the matter differs: immutably on matters that concern our communion with God, and to some extent mutably on matters that concern our communion with one another. This does not mean, he says, that all ceremonies of the church are at the whim of human discretion—certainly not the sacraments, since these are instruments of communion with God (even if secondary details of their administration are discretionary). On the contrary, he says, "we have no where altered the laws of Christ farther than in such particularities only as have the nature of things changeable according to the difference of times, places, persons, and other the like circumstances." The church straddles two realms, and in all its key activities, there is "somewhat Christ hath commanded which must be kept till the world's end" and "somewhat there may be added, as the Church shall judge it expedient" (III.11.13).

Finally, it should be noted that in the latter, the liberty of the Church to make laws for itself is at the same time the liberty of the commonwealth to make laws for the Church. How does this work? When he justifies the queen's supremacy over the church, and Parliament's authority to legislate on matters of church polity, how is this not putting the church in bondage to the State? Certainly that is how we might see it today, and indeed that is, to some extent, how his presbyterian opponents saw it, but for Hooker, the very way in which the question is asked betrays a serious misunderstanding. After all, given the way he has defined the visible church, are not the church and the commonwealth the same body of people? "We say that the care of religion being common unto all societies politic, such societies as do embrace the true religion have the name of the Church given unto every of them for distinction from the rest; so that every body politic hath some religion, but the Church that religion which is only true." In other words, every commonwealth professes some religion, and those which profess the Christian religion are thereby churches, since profession of faith in Christ is, as Hooker has said, the only boundary-marker of the church. Moreover, since pretty much every citizen of England at least *professes* faith in Christ, church and commonwealth are, in this case at least, coterminous:

> We hold, that seeing there is not any man of the Church of England but the same man is also a member of the commonwealth; nor any man a member of the commonwealth, which is not also of the Church of England; therefore . . . one and the selfsame multitude may in such sort be both, and is so with us, that no person appertaining to the one can be denied to be also of the other. (VIII.1.2)

If we take Hooker here to be making a claim about each and every individual in England, this might seem to be an overstatement even in his day, but when we consider the importance of *representation* in his thinking, it is easy to see how he reasons this way. Certainly every public representative in

England is, by his definition, a member of the church. Moreover, Hooker is faithful to Luther's doctrine of the universal priesthood to the extent that he considers laymen, such as these parliamentary representatives, or the queen herself, to have a legitimate role in leading and governing the church. As a general rule, they should defer to the wisdom of the clergy in framing laws for the church, but these clergy have no direct legal authority over the church; this, thinks Hooker, would be to retreat to the tyranny of papalism.

We might, at least after a concerted attempt to put ourselves in Hooker's shoes, understand why it is that he wishes to steer so far clear of the Catholic doctrine of the church as a supernatural polity ruled by the clergy. But from what we have said in this chapter, many readers might worry that Hooker has gone too far in the other direction, so naturalizing and humanizing the visible church that it really is no more sacred than any civil institution. In a profoundly perceptive essay, originally delivered as a lecture in honor of Richard Hooker, Oliver O'Donovan remarks,

> The two standing temptations facing all ecclesiology are, in the first place, (i) to imagine there can be a total coincidence of identity and form, so that to be outside the form is to be excluded from the identity Church in every sense. This is the mistake made by those who first coined the saying, *extra ecclesiam nulla salus*; as we understand the identity of the Church more discriminatingly, of course, we can also understand in what sense such a phrase could be true. In the second place, (ii) there is a temptation to dissociate the identity and the outer form, so that either the outer form claims an autonomy quite apart from ecclesial identity or else it appears quite irrelevant—and in fact these two are just moments in the same process, by which the Church becomes an entirely

secular institution and the identity of the Kingdom of Heaven is vested in individual believers alone. Though we may identify the first of these temptations as the characteristically Catholic temptation and the second as the characteristically Protestant temptation, it is important to see that both temptations continually assail us in every tradition of Christian faith and practice.[16]

Does Hooker, then, fall into the second temptation that O'Donovan names here—dissociating the identity and the outer form? Does grace here float free above nature? This would be surprising indeed giving what we have seen about Hooker's understanding of nature and grace, not to mention his reputation for a robust ecclesiology. But to fully explain this latter aspect to Hooker's theology of the church, we must turn to examine his understanding of the sacraments and liturgy.

FOR DISCUSSION

1. Why was the question of which was the "true church" important in the Reformation? Why did it prove problematic?
2. How does Hooker distinguish the visible and invisible churches? Why is this distinction so important?
3. How does Hooker's understanding of the visible church as a "politic society" inform his approach to church government and indeed to civil government?

---

16. "What Kind of Community Is the Church?," 187.

11

KEY THEMES: LITURGY & SACRAMENTS

RECLAIMING RITUAL

IN THE LAST CHAPTER, we saw how for Hooker the spiritual and earthly planes of the church's existence must be rigorously distinguished to avoid a dangerous idealism or legalism. The visible body of professing believers has all the problems that any other human society has, and needs laws of its own, most of which are by their nature flexible in response to the changing needs of the church through history. Taken on its own, these themes which dominate Hooker's exposition of ecclesiology in Book III of his *Laws* might imply that, as a corporate body, the church is nothing but an earthly institution, a collection of sinners and saints who come together for mutual support and perhaps public service, a glorified Rotary Club, rather than the kingdom of heaven.

But there is obviously quite another side to Richard Hooker's theology, one that dominates much of the lengthy Book V of the *Laws,* not to mention Books VI and VII, and which has often been hailed as Hooker's particular contribution to the developing stream of "Anglicanism." If Hooker constructed his ecclesiology in response to the threat of an obsessive attempt to establish visible markers of holiness in the church, he constructed it also in response to the weak apologetic of church leaders like John Whitgift, who seemed unable or unwilling to attribute much positive spiritual value to the visible forms of English worship.

To be sure, Hooker, like Whitgift, laid great stress on the value of order and uniformity. We saw already in the last chapter that for Hooker, as for Whitgift, the church and commonwealth were coextensive and mutually reinforcing, so a well-ordered commonwealth required well-ordered common worship, in which the people signified both their spiritual and political unity by sharing the same liturgy, centered on the practice of common prayer. This "political" purpose of the liturgy, to be sure, was not simply "secular" in the modern sense. Rather, it reflected Hooker's central conviction that "nature hath need of grace, and grace hath use of nature"—that natural earthly practices and institutions, like feast days and solemn ceremonies, were perfected and sacralized by being reoriented toward our true Lord and Savior, as were political institutions as a whole. Indeed, at the outset of his treatment of the liturgy, he declared, "If the course of politic affairs cannot in any good sort go forward without fit instruments, and that which fitteth them be their virtues, let polity acknowledge itself indebted to religion, godliness being the chiefest top and wellspring of all true virtues, even as God is of all good things" (V.1.2).

But Hooker did more than simply flesh out Whitgift's vision of the value of orderly civil religion. Rather than merely affirming the symbolic ceremonies of the English liturgy as lawful and orderly, he gave them a positive role in the dynamic edification of the Christian community, responding to the Puritan demand for "edifying" church practices. Peter Lake finds this turn profoundly significant, representing "the reclamation of the whole realm of symbolic action and ritual practice from the status of popish superstition to that of a necessary, indeed essential, means of communication and edification; a means, moreover, in many ways more effective than the unvarnished word."[1]

Moreover, Lake finds great significance in the fact that "Hooker thus went out of his way to emphasize that the sacraments had real objective effects; not mere signs, they really did confer grace."[2] From this, along with Hooker's vivid language of *participation* in Book V, where he speaks of the church's union with Christ, Lake concludes that "symbol and ritual were able to play a central role in that process whereby the church led the believer toward union with God,"[3] and that

> Hooker's insistence on the need to rely on the means which God had ordained to unite us with him in Christ also tended to conflate the two levels of the church's existence. . . . For the incorporation of the believer into that mystical body which was the invisible church was linked directly to his entry into the visible church. Incorporation into the one society led to incorporation into the other.[4]

If Lake's reading is right, it is no wonder that later Laudians and even the Oxford Movement would claim Hooker as their inspiration. But we should know enough already to be suspicious of this reading. Sure enough, Lake's quotations from Hooker do not always match his paraphrases:

1. *Anglicans and Puritans*, 165.
2. Ibid., 174.
3. Ibid., 169.
4. Ibid., 180.

on the sacraments, the quote he chooses affirms that the sacraments "represent or signify" grace, but never uses the word "confer";[5] on "entry into the visible church," the passage quoted speaks only of "mystical conjunction" and "real adoption."[6] And if Hooker really meant to "*conflate* the two levels of the church's existence," as opposed to merely uniting them, why so rigorously distinguish them in the first place, as we shall see he does below? But, as we noted in the past chapter, Lake is hardly alone in coming up with such a reading, one in which the gap between the two levels of the church's existence is collapsed. Is there a way to do justice to Lake's observations without ignoring the clear distinctions that Hooker is at pains to establish? Thankfully, I think there is.

In several of his writings on Hooker, Torrance Kirby has proposed the logic of Chalcedonian Christology as a framework for understanding many of the dualities that structure Hooker's thought. Given the central position Hooker's own articulation of Christology occupies in the *Laws*, this certainly makes sense. Hooker notes that for classical Christian theology, Christ is is *truly* God, *perfectly* man, *indivisibly* both in one person, and yet *distinctly* both in two natures. The personal union of the two natures never entails conflating them, or merging them into some third thing. On the contrary, Christ somehow remains simultaneously and perfectly both divine and human, without mixture or confusion.[7] Even as we must in certain contexts rigorously distinguish between the two natures, in other contexts, we may, by a "communication of idioms," affirm of one the attributes of the other.[8] The same logic, argues

---

5. Lake, *Anglicans and Puritans*, 174, quoting *Laws* V.67.5.

6. *Laws* V.56.7.

7. See especially *Laws* V.54.10.

8. See *Laws* V.52.4: "Forasmuch therefore as Christ hath no

Kirby, underlies Hooker's understanding of the Protestant distinction of justification and sanctification: the perfect imputed righteousness by which a believer is wholly righteous in Christ, but not in himself, and the progressively infused righteousness, whereby a believer gradually and partially becomes righteous in his earthly life. These two, for Hooker as for his Protestant predecessors, can neither be separated nor confused. And the same goes for all the other dualities that were linked to the justification/sanctification distinction, including the mystical/visible church distinction. Kirby summarizes:

> Thus membership in the "mystical bodie" of the Church is tied by personal union to participation in the external, visible institution of the Church. In parallel fashion, the Godhead is revealed to man through the mediation of Christ's assumption of the human nature. There is thus, by analogy, an *ecclesiological* 'communication of idioms' between the mystical and institutional Churches, just as in Christology between the human and divine natures.[9]

Although the analogy is limited, I think it does give us a very helpful framework for making sense of Hooker's sharp distinction between the divine/mystical and human/visible sides of the church, and at the same time, his close connection between the two. Indeed, in speaking of the duty of public prayer, he refers to it as an activity we engage in "joined as parts to that visible mystical body which is his Church" (V.24.1), the only place where he thus combines

---

personal subsistence but one whereby we acknowledge him to have been eternally the Son of God, we must of necessity apply to the person of the Son of God even that which is spoken of Christ according to his human nature."

9. Kirby, *Reformer and Platonist*, 93.

the two adjectives.[10] To adequately plumb the depths of this relation would require delving far deeper into Hooker's theology than we can possibly do here, but we can make some progress by singling out two key elements: Hooker's doctrine of *correspondences*, and his doctrine of *participation*. At the risk of serious oversimplification, we may associate the first with his theology of worship generally, the second with his account of the sacraments in particular.

DOCTRINE OF CORRESPONDENCES

Peter Lake's first mistake, in fact, is to fail to distinguish these two. To be sure, he was hardly the first to make this mistake. When John Whitgift attempted to defend the use of rings in a wedding ceremony on the basis of their symbolic value, Thomas Cartwright protested in a flash that this was "to institute new sacraments."[11] Hooker thinks that this objection has misunderstood the key function of a sacrament. This is not to serve as a visible sign of invisible things (for such signs are everywhere in human affairs), or even as a visible sign of specifically spiritual things (for Hooker believes that every creature serves as such a sign of God's presence, manifesting the law of his being through its own law-like operations). Instead, "sacraments are those which are signs and tokens of some general promised grace, which

---

10. On reflection, it is quite appropriate that here, of all places, Hooker should highlight the inseparability of the two dimensions. When we pray, we speak visibly and audibly, and yet believe that our words communicate to one who is invisible, and whose Spirit prays with us, giving voice to our voicelessness. Moreover, our public prayers, although chiefly directed toward God, are at the same time a way of speaking to and admonishing one another in the horizontal communion of saints. Prayer is indeed for Hooker the paradigmatic point at which mystical and visible, heaven and earth come together.

11. Cartwright, *Replie*, 159 (*Whitgift's Works* III:354).

always really descendeth from God unto the soul that duly receiveth them" (IV.1.4). God's "general promise" of grace in the sacraments establishes in their case a special and *necessary* connection between the outward and inward that is lacking in the case of other ceremonies. These may indeed serve to our sanctification, helping us to grow in grace, but remain within the realm of human discretion.

This discretion is not haphazard or arbitrary, though; this is where Hooker goes beyond Whitgift. Since we are creatures of sense, we need sensible aids to help our souls rise to the contemplation of divine things. Accordingly, in establishing the basic principles of his defense of the liturgy, he quotes the Christian neo-Platonist Pseudo-Dionysius: "The sensible things which Religion hath hallowed, are resemblances framed according to things spiritually understood, whereunto they serve as a hand to lead and a guide to direct" (IV.1.3). To fulfill this function, these outward signs, while in no way being confused with the inward realities, ought to resemble and correspond to them. Hooker elaborates in a key passage which warrants close attention:

> If we affect him not far above and before all things, our religion hath not that inward perfection which it should have, neither do we indeed worship him as our God. That which inwardly each man should be, the Church outwardly ought to testify. And therefore the duties of our religion which are seen must be such as that affection which is unseen ought to be. Signs must resemble the things they signify. If religion bear the greatest sway in our hearts, our outward religious duties must show it, as far as the Church hath outward ability. Duties of religion performed by whole societies of men, ought to have in them according to our power a sensible excellency, correspondent to the majesty of him

> whom we worship. Yea then are the public duties of religion best ordered, when the militant Church doth resemble by sensible means, as it may in such cases, the hidden dignity and glory wherewith the Church triumphant in heaven is beautified. (V.6.2)

Accordingly, Hooker will defend the much-maligned white vestments required of priests in Elizabeth's church on the basis that they picture to us the white garments of the angels, worshipping in the presence of God.[12]

By this means, Hooker brings together the "hidden dignity and glory" of the church triumphant with the imperfect worship of the church here on earth. In the act of public worship, the visible church symbolically enacts the believer's inward worship of God, and indeed aids it, serving "as a hand to lead and a guide to direct," but the two planes are not confused. Outward worship in itself, without the active participation of a conscience yearning after God, does no good—at least none beyond the outward order that so preoccupied Whitgift. And if even their effect on our sanctification is not automatic, then certainly they have no direct effect on our standing with God; they are not, as many late medieval Catholic rites had become, prerequisites for warding off God's wrath or earning his favor. Thus, Peter Lake is incautious when he says, "By exploiting and mirroring the correspondences and links between these two realms, symbol and ritual were able to play a central role in that process whereby the church led the believer toward union with God." In one sense, yes, the beautiful and uplifting public worship of the church does lead the believer onward and upward on the path of sanctification and his eventual glorification in the presence of God. In another sense, though, without the believer being united to

12. *Laws* V.39.5.

God and justified by faith, the liturgy will not advance him one step further. Hooker's theology of liturgy, then, while certainly more robust than most of the other Reformers, does not appear to surrender any of their fundamental theological convictions, or protests against the worship of the medieval Church.

DOCTRINE OF PARTICIPATION

Few themes are so fashionable in theology nowadays as "participation." Just look at a catalog of recent theological publications in almost any theological tradition and you will see what I mean. It is difficult to resist the sense that the newfound popularity of this theme owes much to its vagueness, the readiness with which it can be invoked to serve any number of purposes, tying together different theological topics, or creating the illusion of ecumenical convergence, without the hard work of distinction and definition. It also appeals to our postmodern search for "mystery" in a demystified world. But it is, for all that, an important theme in Hooker's thought that warrants discussion here, even if we must begin with some cautionary remarks.

First, it must be said that some treatments of Hooker's doctrine of participation run roughshod over the careful lines he himself seeks to draw as he moves from his treatment of Christology in Book V, chapters 51–55 to his treatment of sacraments in chapters 57–68.[13] Some Orthodox and Catholic theologians (as well as Anglo-Catholics and some more incautious Protestants) will refer to the church, indeed, the visible church, as the extension of the Incarnation, so that our participation in Christ through the sacraments becomes a means of our union with God,

---

13. See for instance the inadequately nuanced discussion in Harrison, "The Church," 305–15.

tantamount to Christ's own hypostatic union. For Hooker, this blurs some key distinctions. The first is laid down clearly in the transitional chapter, chapter 56, where he explains that the union of God and man in Christ Jesus was unique and unrepeatable: "God is not so in any, nor any so in God as Christ. . . . All other things that are of God have God in them and he them in himself likewise. Yet because their substance and his wholly differeth, their coherence and communion either with him or amongst themselves is in no sort like unto that before mentioned" (V.56.4–5). Nonetheless, we are all still capable of a certain kind of union with God, indeed, as believers, a profoundly intimate union through the medium of Christ.

Before coming to this mystical union, however, Hooker notes that in some measure, all of God's creatures participate in God on a metaphysical level, as the source of their life and being: "All things which God hath made are in that respect the offspring of God, they are *in him* as effects are in their highest cause, he likewise actually is *in* them, the assistance and influence of his deity *is their life*" (V.56.5). This sentiment reflects Hooker's neo-Platonic metaphysic, and illustrates his understanding of the relationship of nature and grace that we have mentioned before—just as grace perfects a preexisting inclination toward God in nature, so the mystical union of believers with God as the source of new life perfects a preexisting union of creatures with God as the source of any life.

Hooker's account of this mystical union rests on his predestinarian convictions, but he resists the implication (present in some forms of predestinarian theology) that this reduces our union with Christ into a mere intellectual figment of the divine mind or will, as if that union consisted merely in the decree from all eternity to count Christ's merits to our account. Rather, "they which . . . were in God eternally by their intended admission to life, have by vocation or adoption God actually now in them. . . . Our being in Christ by eternal foreknowledge saveth us not without our actual and real adoption into the fellowship of his saints in this present world" (V.56.7). Although predestination lies outside of all time, it takes effect in time, as each of us is effectually called and grafted into the mystical body of Christ. Hooker speaks of this union in very rich and realistic terms:

> His body crucified and his blood shed for the life of the world, are the true elements of that heavenly being, which maketh us such as himself is of whom we come. For which cause the words of Adam may be fitly the words of Christ concerning his Church, *Flesh of my flesh and bone of my bones*, a true native extract out of mine own body. So that in him even according to his manhood we according to our heavenly being are as branches in that root out of which they grow. (V.56.7)

The line "even according to his manhood" is crucial for Hooker, as it was for Calvin, whose theology he follows closely in this section of the *Laws*. He explicitly critiques any understanding of union with Christ which makes it to be a mere union of our souls with Christ's divine nature. "For doth any man doubt but that even from the flesh of Christ our very bodies do receive that life which shall make them glorious at the later day, and for which they are already accounted parts of his blessed body? . . . Christ is therefore both as God and as man that true vine whereof we both spiritually and corporally are branches." This is strange language to most of us today, though not to the Patristic writers whom Hooker quotes heavily in this section. For them, as for Hooker, our resurrection at the last day is not as it were some sudden miracle of divine power wrought out of the blue, but the fruition of the incorruptible life which our very bodies have received from their union with the already-resurrected body of Christ. Not, to be sure, that there is any "mixture of his bodily substance with ours" but there is a "mystical conjunction [by which we] receive from that vital efficacy which we know to be in his" (V.56.9).

However, all of what we have treated thus far remains at the level of what Hooker calls the "mystical," that is, the invisible. Some scholars have mistakenly read V.56 as if Hooker is already talking about the sacraments and the visible church, so that outward ceremonies themselves can accomplish this new life in God.[14] But at this point Hooker is still speaking only of soteriology, not of sacramentology or even ecclesiology per se, and he notes that our union with Christ takes the twofold form of extrinsic justification and intrinsic sanctification: "Thus we participate Christ partly by imputation, as when those things which he did and suffered for us are imputed unto us for righteousness; partly by habitual and real infusion, as when grace is inwardly bestowed while we are on earth" (V.56.11). How then do sacraments, the visible rituals of the visible body of Christ, contribute to our participation in Christ? This Hooker turns to tackle in the next chapter.

THE NECESSITY OF SACRAMENTS

Hooker is insistent that, mysterious though the subject may be, we must not take refuge in a rationalism that gives the sacraments no function but "*to teach* the mind, by other senses, that which the word doth teach by hearing" (V.57.1). To be sure, they do teach a great deal, and serve as "provocations to godliness, preservations from sin, memorials of

---

14. So Lake, *Anglicans and Puritans*, 180, and even Kirby, *Reformer and Platonist*, 109.

the principal benefits of Christ" among many other benefits. But this is not all. Beyond all this,

> they are heavenly ceremonies, which God hath sanctified and ordained to be administered in his Church, first as marks whereby to know when God doth impart the vital or saving grace of Christ unto all that are capable thereof, and secondly as means conditional which God requireth in them unto whom he imparteth grace. (V.57.3)

Like most of Hooker's definition statements, every word here is carefully chosen. To understand the significance of Hooker's formulation here, it may be helpful to situate it against the taxonomy made popular by Brian Gerrish in his study of Calvin's sacramentology. Gerrish notes that in the Reformed tradition, we find at least three distinct sacramental doctrines (particularly with respect to the Eucharist): *symbolic memorialism*, in which the elements are symbols that serve as an occasion to publicly declare and remember the work of Christ, *symbolic parallelism*, in which the elements are symbols that signify that God is simultaneously but invisibly bestowing the grace of union with Christ upon worthy recipients, and *symbolic instrumentalism*, in which the elements actually serve somehow as the instruments through which God bestows that grace upon worthy recipients.[15] The first appears to have been the doctrine of Zwingli, and became prevalent in many Protestant churches from the nineteenth century onward; the second, that of his successor Bullinger and many other Reformed divines; the third, that of Calvin and many influenced by him.

---

15. Gerrish, *Grace and Gratitude*, 167.

Although Hooker was of course unaware of Gerrish's taxonomy, he was no doubt aware of Calvin and Bullinger's struggles to find mutually satisfactory language on this point, and it is not a stretch to see him in this chapter striving to provide a clearly defined formulation that reconciles *symbolic parallelism* and *symbolic instrumentalism* (having clearly rejected *symbolic memorialism* as inadequate, even if it is clearly a part of what the sacraments involve). So we note that the first part of his definition clearly expresses parallelism: "marks whereby to know when God doth impart the vital or saving grace of Christ." Here, it is clearly *God* who does the imparting, and the sacraments serve simply as marks to tell us when. Hooker does not back down on this point, forthrightly rejecting any concept of an *ex opere operato* efficacy to sacraments in the exposition that follows: "grace is a consequent of sacraments . . . a benefit which he that hath receiveth from God himself the author of sacraments and not from any other natural or supernatural quality in them"; "they contain in *themselves* no vital force or efficacy"; "for all receive not the grace of God which receive the sacraments of his grace"; "which grace also they that receive by sacraments or with sacraments, receive it from him and not from them" (V.57.4). This includes also the conviction, implied in Hooker's proviso that sacraments "impart the vital or saving grace of Christ *unto all that are capable thereof*" that sacraments do not simply impart grace automatically to every recipient, but only to those who, by God's good pleasure, are made capable of receiving by faith.

Hooker, however, is willing to go beyond parallelism and speak of an instrumentalism, if carefully defined. Hence the second part of his definition, that sacraments are "means conditional which God requireth in them unto whom he imparteth grace." In other words, not merely does God freely bestow grace alongside the sacraments, but he has so ordered the economy of redemption that the grace thereby bestowed is made contingent on our faithful reception of them: "neither is it *ordinarily* his will to bestow the grace of the sacraments on any, but by the sacraments" (V.57.4, emphasis Hooker's). From this standpoint, they may be spoken of as instruments, not because there is anything in the sacraments themselves that makes them effectual in this regard, but simply because God has chosen to designate them as prerequisites, as it were, for pouring out his grace.

> It may be hereby both understood that sacraments are necessary, and that the manner of their necessity to life supernatural is not in all respects as food unto natural life, because they contain in *themselves* no vital force or efficacy, they are not physical but *moral instruments* of salvation, duties of service and worship, which unless we perform as the author of grace requireth, they are unprofitable. (V.57.4, emphasis Hooker's)[16]

A very down-to-earth example may serve to clarify what Hooker wants to highlight here. Suppose I make my son's $5 allowance contingent on his cleaning the garage weekly. Clearly, there is nothing intrinsic to the action of cleaning the garage that entails the grace of receiving $5, but once I have designated it as a "means conditional" to the allowance, it becomes ordinarily necessary to that end. Moreover, perhaps I require also that my son demonstrate a joyful attitude, displaying his recognition that he is part of our family and wants to contribute to it. So Hooker too believes that not just any reception, but a *faithful* reception of the sacraments is necessary for us to receive the grace that

---

16. For a more in-depth treatment, see Hooker's careful discussion in Laws VI.6.9-11.

attends them. To be sure, the sacraments are for Hooker no such crass transaction, but an extraordinary display of grace whereby we receive not just the benefits of Christ's death, but the participation in his life, and through it, the life of God himself. But in order to preserve the very gratuity of the sacraments, it is crucial to Hooker to maintain that the grace remains in the hand of the divine giver, not in the "moral instrument": "For of sacraments the very same is true which Solomon's wisdom observeth in the brazen serpent, 'He that turned towards it was not healed by the thing he saw, but by thee O Lord'" (V.57.4).[17]

This careful formulation establishes the basis upon which Hooker is willing to use the language of "instruments" or "causes" of grace in relation to the sacraments, and it is unfortunate that so many readers of Hooker have read the expositions on baptism and the Eucharist without first digesting the definitions he lays down in V.57. These definitions enable Hooker to consistently make three points throughout his exposition of baptism and the Eucharist: (1) to be sure, God *can*, and in extraordinary cases *does*, give sacramental grace without the administration and reception of the sacraments; (2) however, given his clear commands to us to observe the sacraments, we have no business testing him, but must make it our first priority to receive (and, in the case of clergy, to administer) the sacraments; (3) since the sacraments are not "physical instruments," we must receive them with faith in order to enjoy the promised benefits.[18]

---

17. Hooker quotes here from the apocryphal Wisdom of Solomon 16:7.

18. It is worth noting in this regard that when it comes to the Eucharist, Hooker is unambiguously receptionist—that is, there is no gracious change, nor presence of Christ, in the elements as such, but only in the faithful receiver. This would seem so clear as to be unworthy of comment except for the fact that a striking number of Hooker scholars have asserted the opposite (see for instance, Harrison, "The

What then are these promised benefits? We know already from V.56 that they must pertain to the mystical life-giving union with the incarnate Christ, so vividly described there. But is there any difference between baptism and the Eucharist? Yes. "We receive Christ Jesus in baptism once as the first beginner, in the Eucharist often as being by continual degrees the finisher of our life" (V.57.6). Having cautioned clearly against putting too much stock in the elements themselves, Hooker feels free to speak in very strong terms of what God intends to accomplish by means of our reception of them. Regarding baptism, Hooker elaborates that by it we are "incorporated into Christ and so through his most precious merit obtain as well that saving grace of imputation which taketh away all former guiltiness, as also that infused divine virtue of the holy Ghost which giveth to the powers of the soul their first disposition towards future newness of life"; that it is "the door of our actual entrance into God's house, the first apparent beginning of life, a seal perhaps to the grace of *election* before received, but to our

---

Church," 313; David Neelands, one of the few to unambiguously assert Hooker's receptionism, also offers a catalogue of other offenders in this regard in his "Christology and the Sacraments," 383n69). This is a good example of what I said in chapter 4, about many interpreters assuming that since Hooker is an "Anglican" he must say what "Anglicans" are supposed to say, even when he clearly doesn't. A few passages will suffice: "The real presence of Christ's most blessed body and blood is not therefore to be sought for in the sacrament, but in the worthy receiver of the sacrament." "I see not which way it should be gathered by the words of Christ when and where the bread is his body or the cup his blood but only in the very heart and soul of him which receiveth them. As for the sacraments, they really exhibit, but for aught we can gather out of that which is written of them they are not really nor do really contain in themselves that grace which with them or by them it pleaseth God to bestow." "There is no sentence of holy scripture which saith that we cannot by this sacrament be made partakers of his body and blood except they be first contained in the sacrament or the sacrament converted into them" (all from V.67.6).

sanctification here a step that hath not any before it" (V.60.2, 3).[19] Regarding the Eucharist, Hooker elaborates, "They which by baptism have laid the foundation and attained the first beginning of a new life have here their nourishment and food prescribed for *continuance* of life in them. Such as will live the life of God must eat the flesh and drink the blood of the Son of Man, because this is a part of that diet which if we want we cannot live" (V.67.1).

A EUCHARISTIC ECUMENISM

Hookers's exposition of the Eucharist in chapter 67 of Book V is justly accounted as one of the greatest sections of the *Laws*, or perhaps of all English theological literature, and I would do better to simply direct the reader to read it in full, rather than seeking to walk through it here, especially as this chapter is already long. But I do want to close by highlighting a feature of it that reflects his theological method generally, which ought to still commend his work to us today.

Hooker is well aware that no issue had been the source of such discord and indeed violence in the sixteenth century as the doctrine of the Eucharist. As large as the issues of justification by faith or sola Scriptura loom in hindsight when we consider the battle-lines of the Reformation, we can often forget that if Protestants were burned at the stake,

---

19. Hooker does not, alas, explain how to reconcile this saving grace given to all who are baptized with the fact that clearly not all the baptized are saved in the end. Clearly for Hooker, apostasy from a state of initial justification is a real possibility, even if the elect will surely persevere to the end. The thorny questions regarding the relationship of sacramental grace, election, and apostasy that were to trouble the Reformed in the seventeenth century, had not yet been pressed as forcefully as they would soon be, and although Hooker's *Dublin Fragments* might have given us a fuller exposition on the issue, they never came close to completion.

it was usually because of their refusal to affirm transubstantiation. And if Protestants were dividing from one another and calling each other nasty names, it was usually because of rival understandings (or misunderstandings of one another's understandings) of Christ's eucharistic presence. Hooker thus frames his chapter on the Eucharist, penned toward the very end of the tumultuous sixteenth century, as a call to put aside all such bitterness and get back to the point of the sacrament. Of course, we have already seen enough to know that this irenical overture is not the result of any theological woolliness, a refusal to worry about any of the relevant distinctions; Hooker is well aware of the need for careful definitions where the sacraments are involved. But the main point of such definitions is to keep us from trying to transgress the mystery, arrogantly insisting that we have it figured out, and everyone else must accept our formulation.

Accordingly, Hooker begins his account by trying to highlight what nearly all the warring doctrines have in common. He takes for granted that all parties in his day are agreed in rejecting Zwinglianism,[20] in which the sacrament is "a shadow, destitute, empty, and void of Christ." The Reformed then (whether Bullingerian or Calvinistic), the Lutheran, and indeed the Catholics are all agreed in affirming a "*real participation* of Christ and of life in his body and blood *by means of this sacrament*" so "wherefore should the world continue still distracted, and rent with so manifold contentions, when there remaineth now no controversy saving only about the subject *where* Christ is?" Indeed, all parties agree that "the *soul of man* is the receptacle of Christ's presence" (V.67.2, emphasis Hooker's), so that the

---

20. An intriguing remark, given that much secondary literature today continues to mistakenly claim that Zwinglianism was a dominant doctrine in the Elizabethan Church, especially among Puritans.

disagreement only concerns whether the presence is *only* there (as the Reformed say) or also somehow in the bread and wine (as the Lutherans and Catholics say in their own distinctive ways). What a foolish debate! laments Hooker. "I wish that men would more give themselves to meditate with silence what we have by the sacrament, and less to dispute of the manner how. . . . Curious and intricate speculations do hinder, they abate, they quench such inflamed motions of delight and joy as divine graces use to raise" (V.67.3).

This is not the anti-intellectual's throwing up of the hands and saying, "Oh, who cares about these abstract speculations; let's just agree to disagree!" Indeed, Hooker takes some time to explain why it is that the Reformed doctrine conveys all that Scripture and patristic reason require, and makes clear that he deems both Lutheran consubstantiation and Catholic transubstantiation to be confusing, baseless, and contrary to reason (though he does not object to people believing these doctrines, so much as insisting on the necessity of others believing them, as the Lutherans and Catholics had). Rather, what we have in this chapter is Hooker the pastor showing his concern for how, by turning the sacraments into an object of disputation rather than grateful wonder, his contemporaries had deprived ordinary believers of the benefits God had in store for them. He ends the chapter in a beautiful peroration that invites his hearers to put aside all vain speculation and dispute and instead take, eat, and be thankful:

> Let it therefore be sufficient for me presenting myself at the Lord's table to know what there I receive from him, without searching or inquiring of the manner how Christ performeth his promise; let disputes and questions, enemies to piety, abatements of true devotion and hitherto in this cause but over-patiently heard, let them

take their rest . . . what these elements are in themselves it skilleth [matters] not, it is enough that to me which take them they are the body and blood of Christ, his promise in witness hereof sufficeth, his word he knoweth which way to accomplish, why should any cogitation possess the mind of a faithful communicant but this, "O my God thou art true, O my soul thou art happy"? (V.67.12)

FOR DISCUSSION

1. Why is Hooker's emphasis on sacraments important, according to Peter Lake? What are some problems with Lake's reading?
2. What is Hooker's doctrine of correspondences and how does it inform his approach to liturgy?
3. What is Hooker's doctrine of participation and in what ways does it relate to (and yet remain distinct from) his understanding of sacraments?
4. In what ways is Hooker's approach to sacraments ecumenical without being watered-down or reductionistic?

12

RICHARD HOOKER: CONTEMPORARY

RECOVERING DISCRIMINATION

We live in an age that cannot stand labels. The reflexive "Don't label me" of the rebellious teenager has become a motto for our generation. Everyone wants the freedom to carve out their own identity. To many modern readers, the considerable effort expended in this book to label Hooker's theological identity, and his viewpoint on various topics, might well seem like a waste of time. Why not just let him be his own man—neither "Reformed," "Anglican," "Calvinist," "Arminian," or anything else? But Hooker would have been the first to point out that we cannot very well do without labels, something that we find today in the curious paradox that our culture is obsessed with labeling even as it complains about it, cooking up a new label for the myriad of new identities we try and generate for ourselves. Whether in politics, religion, or sexuality, it seems, one now has to identify oneself in relation to an alphabet soup of different orientations and movements. And for all our insistence on freedom in shaping our identity, once shaped, we guard it jealously—as evidenced by that new term that has recently entered our language and that makes havoc of our societies, "identity politics."

It is telling that the word "discrimination," which used to be considered a virtue, is now wholly negative in connotation. To understand the difference between one thing and another, to draw relevant distinctions, refusing to blur important boundaries between objectively different things—all of this is essential to politics, to law, to theology, and to thought in general. But today, we are inclined to deconstruct any such claims to objective distinction as just so much subjective prejudice. Richard Hooker, a master of discrimination, knew better: "The mixture of those things by speech which by nature are divided, is the mother of all error. To take away therefore that error which confusion breedeth, distinction is requisite. Rightly to distinguish is by conceit of mind to sever things different in nature, and to discern wherein they differ" (III.3.1).

We have seen Hooker at work in this task of discrimination throughout our brief survey here: discriminating between nature and grace, visible and invisible, justification and sanctification, between different kinds of certainty, different kinds of law, different aspects of the church, different theories of the sacraments. And all of this discrimination, far from being a mere exercise in logic-chopping, enables Hooker, he thinks, to "resolve the consciences" of his readers—to dispel doubts, to forestall conflicts, to provide a sound basis for harmonious public action. If we are to learn from Richard Hooker today, perhaps this is the best place to start—to learn from him the difficult business of "severing things different in nature."

It is symptomatic, perhaps, of how far we have declined, that many readers of Hooker would rather not go to this trouble. We have noted already in this book any number of places where scholars summarizing Hooker are considerably less clear than Hooker himself, blurring together categories that he labors to distinguish. But we have seen also, on a larger level, scholars who are not even sure it is the historian's task to discriminate—between true and false assertions, good and bad arguments. We noted A. J. Joyce brushing aside as apparently irrelevant the question of whether Hooker makes *true* accusations against his opponents. We noted Peter Lake stating boldly, that the historian's task is "not to adjudicate these disputes" but to maintain a "skeptical relativism."

The posture Lake recommends, while perhaps understandable for an early modern historian, has become the default posture of many of our theologians and churchmen too. "Judge not, lest you be judged," is perhaps our favorite Bible verse. Hooker, to be sure, had plenty of choice words for Puritan leaders who were quick to jump to judgment upon their authorities, and even their brothers' souls, and yet few virtues are so frequently praised in the *Laws* as that of *judgment*. This might not sit well with the dovish picture of Hooker as conciliator and reconciler, occupations that we tend to think of as requiring a fair bit of fuzziness and compromise. Of course, we have seen well enough that this picture is one-sided at best; Hooker is a sharp and effective polemicist, and is not at all interested in reconciliation between truth and error. And yet it remains true that Hooker is no mere partisan; he has much more important objectives in mind than merely winning an argument or vindicating a particular theological position. It remains true, in short, that if one is looking for a relatively conciliating voice from the contentious sixteenth century, Hooker's easily stands out from the pack. Despite being far more interested in discrimination and judgment than his twenty-first-century successors, Hooker is an ecumenist of sorts, a valuable resource for a deeply divided church today trying to learn how to peacefully sort through its differences.

COMMUNITY, IDENTITY, AND HISTORY

So how can Hooker be both judge and reconciler? Today we seemed condemned to choose between either judging and dividing or withholding judgment in order to get along. Two aspects of Hooker's understanding of the world are worth highlighting. First, Hooker is unafraid of corporate identity. We may have gained much in the emergence of individual liberties over the past four centuries, but we have clearly lost much as well. We have lost the sense of ourselves as part of a larger whole within which we find meaning and in whose priorities we can rest without having to decide everything anew for ourselves. We bitterly resist the idea that our identity is conferred on us by our family or place or church or even national history; it is ours to remake as we wish. Of course, we have found to our chagrin that such radical individualism is not as easy as it sounds; humans naturally crave community, as Hooker well recognized, and if they throw off the claims and constraints of the community in which they are born, they will find some other community of meaning to attach themselves to. But here's the catch. Because this new community is chosen rather than given, forged rather than received, it often acquires a militant zeal and defensiveness, defining itself in opposition to all others, vigorously policing dissent, and often presenting itself as the only viable future. We see this today at both ends of the cultural spectrum. On the one hand, no sooner has the gay rights movement (a paradigmatic instance of "identity politics") won its campaign for tolerance and respect than it has turned violently on all rival communities of value, demanding no tolerance at all for traditionalist views of marriage. On the other hand, conservative denominations of all stripes, or transdenominational "movements" defined by a celebrity pastor or guru, readily develop a mass psychology defined by "insiders" and "outsiders," "orthodox" and "apostates," reacting fiercely to dissent and sustaining a delusional optimism about their own importance on the global religious scene.

Richard Hooker, as we have seen, diagnosed this social pathology right at the outset of the *Laws*. Commenting wryly on the religious scene in Switzerland at the time of Calvin (and no doubt with an eye toward the mindset of Puritanism in England):

> Every particular church did that within itself, which some few of their own thought good, by whom the rest were all directed.... But a greater inconvenience it bred, that every later endeavoured to be certain degrees more removed from conformity with the Church of Rome, than the rest before had been; whereupon grew marvelous great dissimilitudes, and by reason thereof, jealousies, heartburnings, jars and discords amonst them. (Pref. 2.2)

The problem that Hooker lays his finger upon here is a common one, but always destructive in social and political life. As Augustine famously observed in the *City of God*, and Oliver O'Donovan has masterfully expounded in our own day, communities must be defined around a *common object of love*; without such, they are not communities at all, but merely a chaotic herd of individuals who have congregated together for safety. Often, however, a community can substitute a common object of fear or hatred for a common object of love. Such a community is defined less by what they all value and hope to accomplish (although they may indeed share positive values) and more by their fear of outsiders or desire to be as unlike them as possible. To be sure, in the sixteenth century, there were many good reasons for Protestants to be afraid of Catholics and want to distance themselves from them, but such fear could never be a sustainable basis for a vibrant church, much less a system of government, as the Presbyterians hoped to create. (The unsustainability of such an ethos of paranoia was quickly proved in the tumultuous years of the English Civil War, when the Puritans finally got their turn to try and govern.)

Hooker's answer to such a militant sense of identity, forged in conflict with the other, the oppressor, the persecutor, is a sense of identity rooted in history. This appeal to history is how Hooker's vision of the church acquires such capacious breadth (encompassing, you will recall, not merely Catholics but heretics and schismatics of all sorts) without sacrificing depth. The depth comes not from the contemporary moment, which can only sustain the necessary depth of meaning by a ferocious stress on purity, but from the long legacy of custom and tradition. For Hooker, the common object of love that sustained his vision of an English church and civil community was the whole cultural inheritance that Elizabethan England had received, an inheritance that included not merely the triumphs of the Protestant Reformers, but the great edifice of medieval scholasticism (which, for all its errors, nonetheless offered countless lasting theological treasures), of the English legal tradition, of the early church, and the great classical heritage that had nourished the Fathers and the medievals. The result was no narrow jingoistic nationalism, but a striking cosmopolitanism—Hooker could certainly say, with Terence, *humani nihil a me alienum puto* ("I do not consider anything human alien to me")—that was nonetheless deeply rooted in the particularity of the Elizabethan experience.

Of course, communities founded on identity with the past can easily become pathological as well: resistant to change, fearful of newcomers, irrationally defensive of obsolete institutions. Such is the standing criticism of political and cultural conservatism. Hooker was certainly a conservative—we need only remember the opening sentence of the *Laws*—and has, as we know, been criticized for undue allegiance to the status quo. But the vision of the *Laws*, as we have seen, is marked far more by its flexibility than its rigidity. While asking us to defer as a general rule to longstanding customs and conventions, Hooker repeatedly insists on the importance of rewriting or discarding obsolete old laws. Laws are "instruments to rule by," and if that which they have to rule has changed, then so must the instrument. The identity which the past confers upon us does not weigh heavily on our shoulders, or confine us like a straitjacket, in Hooker's philosophy of history; rather, it simply equips us with the tools to function effectively in new settings. Perhaps part of how Hooker can simultaneously sustain this reverence *and* looseness towards the past is the very capaciousness of the past he seeks to recover. Any community that clings doggedly to a narrow old tradition of orthodoxy in the face of persecution, that prides itself on being heir to the "faithful few" (we might think of Scots Covenanters, for instance) will be more likely to feel imprisoned rather than liberated by its historical identity. It certainly will not be able to cope well with change, change that may require it to shed elements of that identity. However, a community founded, as Hooker's ideal community was, on Jewel, Luther, Calvin, and Vermigli, on Aquinas and Anselm, Augustine and Athanasius, Aristotle and Cicero, not to mention centuries of national law and custom, could afford to be more flexible. If one's inheritance is vast, one need not fear the loss of any particular portion of it; such a community can change in changing times, without wholly losing its identity.

Hooker thus models for us how it might be possible to embrace a particular identity, an identity one did not even choose for oneself, without either feeling trapped in it, or using it as a weapon against every other community.

ESSENTIALS AND NON-ESSENTIALS

But of course, another element is needed to complete this picture. How can one know, after all, which elements of that identity, which rules and beliefs that sustain your community, can be changed without destroying that identity? It may be true that Hooker's model of a catholic reformed English church could indeed change in changing times without ceasing to be true to itself, but how much? Identities, traditions, and communities are not endlessly elastic, as liberal mainline Protestantism has discovered to its chagrin: change your church enough to accommodate a changing world, and eventually people stop recognizing it as a church at all, and stop showing up. Surely there have to be some nonnegotiable essentials, some core beliefs and practices that provide the backbone of any institution or tradition, and without which it can no longer claim continuity with its past? And yet at the same time, clearly the pathology of many exclusive communities is an insistence that their every characteristic is constitutive, that they cannot be at all without clinging doggedly to each belief and practice as a *sine qua non* of orthodoxy. Within such a community, there is no human law—only divine law. We see this if we continue the passage quoted above, on the divisiveness of the Swiss Reformed churches:

> Their quarrels still might have easily been prevented, if the orders, which each Church did think fit and convenient for itself, had not so peremptorily been established under that high commanding form, which tendered them unto the people, as things everlastingly required by the law of that Lord of lords, against whose statutes there is no exception to be taken. For by this mean it came to pass, that one Church could not but accuse and condemn another of disobedience to the will of Christ, in those things where manifest difference was between them: whereas the selfsame orders allowed, but yet established in more wary and suspense manner, as being to stand in force till God should give the opportunity of some general conference what might be best for every of them afterwards to do; this I say had both prevented all occasion of just dislike which others might take, and reserved a greater liberty unto the authors themselves of entering into farther consultation afterwards. Which though never so necessary they could not easily now admit, without some fear of derogation from their credit: and therefore that which once they had done, they became for ever after resolute to maintain. (Pref. 2.2)

It is for this reason that perhaps the most important contribution of Richard Hooker's theological method, of his careful practice of discrimination, was his insistence on discriminating between essentials and nonessentials, changeables and unchangeables. We see this throughout his theory of law, as he refuses to reduce all law either to the unchangeable decree of the divine will or to the arbitrary decree of human authority. All the laws we encounter are rooted, indeed, in the unchanging nature and will of God, indeed, in the very structure of the world he has made, and the demands of our own human nature. To this extent, we are not free to remake ourselves and the world to suit our whims, as many in our present age seem hell-bent on doing. There are fixed moral norms, and fixed spiritual laws; no society can ever legalize murder, and no church can ever preach salvation in any other name than that of Christ Jesus. But at the same time, all the laws that we encounter in our social lives, whether in church or in state, are *human* laws, *positive* laws, specific applications of the norms of justice and righteousness that may well change as circumstances change. Only careful discrimination and judgment can tell us when change is called for, and how far change can take us in a given instance, without compromising the fundamental norm at stake.

We see this discrimination also in his theory of Scripture, where he is at pains to remind us that not all scriptural statements are of the same sort. All of Scripture, to be sure, carries the authority of God and demands our respect, but it does not all demand our faith and obedience in the same sense. Much of Scripture teaches us truths supernatural, but much teaches us only of natural matters—sometimes enjoining moral principles, other times merely giving prudential counsel (such as Proverbs), or particular legal applications for a certain time and place (such as Deuteronomy), or morally-freighted narratives for our instruction (such as Kings and Chronicles). We must receive each of these for what it is, and apply it properly, with all due discretion. Even direct divine commands are, after all, not necessarily directed directly at us; we must ask who is being commanded, and to what end, before knowing precisely how to apply the Scripture in our own churches and our own experience. Even where we are fairly sure of what scriptural teaching requires, moreover, we ought still to distinguish between those teachings of Scripture central to the Gospel proclamation and those that, while important for our edification and sanctification, are not *sine qua nons* of Christian profession. Such discrimination allows us to argue passionately for the best way of living out our Christian discipleship in particular churches, without thereby excommunicating all others.

Indeed, Hooker's discrimination between essentials and nonessentials, as we have seen, is foundational to his ecclesiology as well. Hooker's invisible church is defined by one essential, which we cannot see—union with the risen Christ. His visible church is defined by one essential, which we can see, but not judge the truth of—profession of faith in the risen Christ. Beyond this, there are many levels of relative necessity—preaching, the sacraments, good discipline, appropriate church government, etc.—none of which Hooker marginalizes as simply unimportant. On the contrary, he will argue forcefully and at length for his position on the role of each, but always contextualized within a careful assessment of what is essential, and in what sense.

Not that any of this discrimination is easy. We might protest, "Sure, it's all well and good to say that everyone will get along better if we just distinguish between essentials and nonessentials; but everyone has a different view of which is which!" Of course, to this one might respond that even just calling us to the task of discrimination is hardly idle within this day and age. Many of us, I think, rarely take the time at all to seriously try and distinguish which aspect of our identities, our moral and theological and political commitments, are really constitutive and essential, and which are ancillary. To be sure, if we did take the time to do so, it would hardly resolve every dispute, but it would make those that remained far easier to navigate. But Hooker is well aware that the task of human judgment and discretion, to which he constantly summons us, is inevitably flawed and messy. *Certainty*, that pot of gold at the end of the rainbow which so many in his generation were seeking (and still so many in ours, despite our loud protestations of skepticism), is precious hard to come by. Sure, Hooker thinks, we can get a bit more successful in our quest if we tighten up our reasoning, demanding sound logic in our own arguments and those of others, and thus arriving, from time to time, at truths that can be demonstrated beyond reasonable doubt. But for the most part, he thinks, we don't solve the problem of certainty by trying harder to achieve it, but by asking ourselves just how much certainty we really need in order to function effectively in the tasks and communities God has called us to. Hooker is no relativist or skeptic—that is abundantly clear. He believes that we can, more often than not, arrive at very good approximations of fixed truth, but for the most part, approximations only. We cannot know with infallible certainty that Julius Caesar was a real person, but that certainly does not keep us from teaching about him in history class. Nor need our considerably greater uncertainty about just what might be the best laws prevent us from submitting to the probable wisdom of the laws currently in place. Our minds must go "which way greatest probability leadeth," but they need not go further than that, and we must have the humility to recognize that when our own private judgment contrasts with a wide consensus, it is probably not all that probable that the truth resides alone in our little heads.

If the contemporary church can learn anything from the wisdom of Richard Hooker, then, I hope that it can learn this extraordinary balance of exclusion and inclusion, of dogmatism and relativism, of history and change, of authority and freedom, of certainty and doubt that gives the *Laws of Ecclesiastical Polity* "such seeds of eternity . . . that shall last till the last fire consume all learning."

FOR DISCUSSION

1. Do you agree that our society and our churches have difficulty making judgments? Why or why not?

2. How does Hooker's understanding of historical community guard against the dangers of identity politics?

3. Do you find Hooker's distinction of essentials and non-essentials to be helpful? Why or why not?

BIBLIOGRAPHY

Note: *If you would like to learn more about Hooker, there are many good sources for further reading. But which ones? Though there is not space to include it here, on my website you will find an extensive annotated bibliography (which I hope to continue adding to) which will hopefully help guide you through the jungle of Hooker studies: http://bradlittlejohn.com/richard-hooker/richard-hooker-annotated-bibliography.*

Almasy, Rudolph P. "They Are and Are Not Elymas: The 1641 'Causes' Notes as Postscript to Richard Hooker's *Of the Lawes of Ecclesiasticall Politie*." In McGrade, ed., *Richard Hooker and the Construction of Christian Community*, 183–202.

———. "Rhetoric and Apologetics." In Kirby, ed., *A Companion to Richard Hooker*, 121–50.

Althusius, Johannes. *On Law and Power*. Translated by Jeffrey J. Veenstra. Sources in Early Modern Economics, Ethics, and Law. Grand Rapids: Christian's Library Press, 2013.

———. *Politica Methodice Digesta* (1603). Reprinted as *The Politics of Johannes Althusius*. Translated and edited by Frederick S. Carney. London: Eyre and Spottiswoode, 1965.

Aquinas, Thomas. *Summa Theologiae*. Translated by the Fathers of the English Dominican Province. New Advent, www.newadvent.org.

Archer, Stanley. *Richard Hooker*. Boston: Twayne, 1983.

Armstrong, Brian G. *Calvinism and the Amyraut Heresy: Protestant Scholasticism and Humanism in Seventeenth-Century France*. Madison: University of Wisconsin Press, 1969.

Bibliography

Atkinson, Nigel. *Richard Hooker and the Authority of Scripture, Tradition and Reason: Reformed Theologian of the Church of England?* Vancouver: Regent College Publishing, 2005.

Avis, P. D. L. *Anglicanism and the Christian Church*. 2nd ed. London: T. & T. Clark, 2002.

———. *The Church in the Theology of the Reformers*. Atlanta: John Knox, 1981.

———. *In Search of Authority: Anglican Theological Method from the Reformation to the Enlightenment*. London: Bloomsbury, 2014.

———. "Moses and the Magistrate: A Study in the Rise of Protestant Legalism." *Ecclesiastical History* 149 (1975) 148–72.

———. Review of *A Companion to Richard Hooker*, edited by Torrance Kirby. *Ecclesiology* 8 (2012) 416–20.

———. "The True Church in Reformation Theology." *Scottish Journal of Theology* 30.4 (1977) 319–45.

Ballor, Jordan J., and W. Bradford Littlejohn. "European Calvinism: Church Discipline." In Irene Dingel and Johannes Paulmann, eds., *European History Online* (EGO). Mainz: Institute of European History (IEG), 2013. http://www.ieg-ego.eu/en/threads/crossroads/religious-and-confessional-spaces/jordan-ballor-w-bradford-littlejohn-european-calvinism-church-discipline.

Bancroft, Richard. *A Sermon preached at Paules Crosse the 8. of Februarie, being the first Sunday in the Parleament, Anno. 1588. by Richard Bancroft D. of Divinitie, and Chaplaine to the right Honorable Sir Christopher Hatton Knight L. Chancelor of England*. London: E. B. [Edward Bollifant] for Gregorie Seton, 1588, i.e., 1589.

Baschera, Luca. "Righteousness Imputed and Inherent: Hooker's Soteriology in the Context of 16th Century Continental Reformed Theology." In Kindred-Barnes and Littlejohn, eds., *Richard Hooker and Reformed Orthodoxy*.

Bauckham, Richard. "Hooker, Travers, and the Church of Rome in the 1580s." *Journal of Ecclesiastical History* 29.1 (1978) 37–50.

Billings, J. Todd. *Calvin, Participation, and the Gift: The Activity of Believers in Union with Christ*. Oxford: Oxford University Press, 2007.

Bozeman, Theodore Dwight. *The Precisianist Strain: Disciplinary Religion & Antinomian Backlash in Puritanism to 1638*. Chapel Hill: University of North Carolina Press, 2004.

Bibliography

Brachlow, Stephen. *The Communion of Saints: Radical Puritan and Separatist Ecclesiology,* 1570–1625. Oxford: Oxford University Press, 1988.

Brydon, Michael. *The Evolving Reputation of Richard Hooker: An Examination of Responses,* 1600–1714. Oxford: Oxford University Press, 2006.

Cartwright, Thomas. *A Replye to an Answere Made of M. Doctor Whitgift . . . Agaynste the Admonition.* s.l., 1574. Reprinted in *Whitgift's Works.*

———. *The Reste of the Second Replie: Agaynst Master Doctor Whitgifts Second Answer Touching the Church Discipline.* Basel: 1577.

———. *The Second Replie of Thomas Cartwright: Agaynst Master Doctor Whitgifts Second Answer Touching the Church Discipline.* Heidelberg: 1575.

Chillingworth, William. *The Religion of Protestants a Safe Way to Salvation* [1637]. London: Thomas Tegg, 1845.

Collinson, Patrick. *The Elizabethan Puritan Movement.* Berkeley: University of California Press, 1967.

———. "Hooker and the Elizabethan Establishment." In McGrade, ed., *Richard Hooker and the Construction of Christian Community,* 149–82.

———. *The Religion of Protestants: The Church in English Society,* 1559–1625. Oxford: Clarendon, 1982.

Compier, Don H. "Hooker on the Authority of Scripture in Matters of Morality." In McGrade, ed., *Richard Hooker and the Construction of Christian Community,* 251–60.

Coolidge, John S. *The Pauline Renaissance in England: Puritanism and the Bible.* Oxford: Clarendon, 1970.

Dominiak, Paul. "Hooker, Scholasticism, and Reformed Orthodoxy." In Kindred-Barnes and Littlejohn, eds., *Richard Hooker and Reformed Orthodoxy.*

Dyson, R. W., ed., trans. *Aquinas: Political Writings.* Cambridge Texts in the History of Political Thought. Cambridge: Cambridge University Press, 2007.

Edelen, Georges. "Hooker's Style." In W. Speed Hill, ed., *Studies in Richard Hooker: Essays Preliminary to an Edition of His Works,* 241–78. Cleveland: Press of Case Western Reserve University, 1972.

Eppley, Daniel. "Practicing What He Preaches? Richard Hooker on the Reform of Ecclesiastical Law." In Kindred-Barnes and Littlejohn, eds., *Richard Hooker and Reformed Orthodoxy.*

Fincham, Kenneth. *Prelate as Pastor: The Episcopate of James I*. Oxford: Clarendon, 1990.

Frere, W. H., and C. E. Douglas, eds. *Puritan Manifestoes: A Study of the Origin of the Puritan Revolt*. London: SPCK, 1907.

Fulford, Andrew. "'A Truth Infallible': Richard Hooker and Reformed Orthodoxy on *Autopistos*." In Kindred-Barnes and Littlejohn, eds., *Richard Hooker and Reformed Orthodoxy*.

Fuller, Thomas. *The Church History of Britain, from the Birth of Jesus Christ until the Year MDCXLVIIII*. 3 vols. 3rd ed. London: Thomas Tegg, 1842.

Gerrish, Brian A. *Grace and Gratitude: The Eucharistic Theology of John Calvin*. Minneapolis: Fortress, 1993.

Gibbs, Lee W. "Richard Hooker: Prophet of Anglicanism or English Magisterial Reformer?" *Anglican Theological Review* 84 (2002) 943–60.

———. "Richard Hooker's *Via Media* Doctrine of Scripture and Tradition." *Harvard Theological Review* 95.2 (2002) 227–35.

Grabill, Stephen J. *Rediscovering the Natural Law in Reformed Theological Ethics*. Emory University Studies in Law and Religion. Grand Rapids: Eerdmans, 2006.

Harrison, William H. "Powers of Nature and Influences of Grace in Hooker's *Lawes*." In Kirby, ed., *Richard Hooker and the English Reformation*, 15–24.

Haugaard, William P. Introduction to books 2, 3 & 4. In W. Speed Hill, ed., *The Folger Library Edition of the Works of Richard Hooker*, vol. 6, *Of the Lawes of Ecclesiastical Politie, Books I–VIII: Introductions and Commentary*. Binghamton, NY: Medieval & Renaissance Texts & Studies, 1993.

Hill, W. Speed, gen. ed. *The Folger Library Edition of the Works of Richard Hooker*. Vols. 1-5. Cambridge, MA: Belknap Press of Harvard University Press, 1977-1990.

- Volume 1. Georges Edelen, ed. *The Folger Library Edition of the Works of Richard Hooker*, vol. 1, *The Laws of Ecclesiastical Polity: Pref., Books I to IV*. Cambridge: Belknap of Harvard University Press, 1977.
- Volume 2. W. Speed Hill, ed. *The Folger Library Edition of the Works of Richard Hooker*, vol. 2, *The Laws of Ecclesiastical Polity: Book V*. Cambridge: Belknap of Harvard University Press, 1977.
- Volume 3. P. G. Stanwood, ed. *The Folger Library Edition of the Works of Richard Hooker*, vol. 3, *The Laws of Ecclesiastical Polity: Books VI, VII, VIII*. Cambridge: Belknap of Harvard University Press, 1981.

Bibliography

Volume 4. John E. Booty, ed. *The Folger Library Edition of the Works of Richard Hooker*, vol. 4, *Of the Lawes of Ecclesiasticall Politie: Attack and Response*. Cambridge: Belknap of Harvard University Press, 1982.

Volume 5. Laetitia Yeandle, ed. *The Folger Library Edition of the Works of Richard Hooker*, vol. 5, *Tractates and Sermons*. Cambridge: Belknap of Harvard University Press, 1990.

Hutchinson, E. J., and Korey Maas. "Niels Hemmingsen (1513–1600) and the Development of Lutheran Natural-Law Teaching." *Journal of Markets & Morality* 17.2 (2014) 595–617.

Ingalls, Ranall. "Sin and Grace." In Kirby, ed., *A Companion to Richard Hooker*, 151–84.

Jacobsen, Ken. "'The Law of a Commonweal': The Social Vision of Hooker's *Of the Laws of Ecclesiastical Polity* and Shakespeare's *The Taming of the Shrew*." *Animus* 12 (2008) 15–28.

Joyce, A. J. *Richard Hooker and Anglican Moral Theology*. Oxford: Oxford University Press, 2012.

Junius, Franciscus. *The Mosaic Polity*. Translated by Todd M. Rester. Sources in Early Modern Economics, Ethics, and Law. Grand Rapids: Christian's Library, 2015.

Keble, John, ed. *The Works of That Learned and Judicious Divine Mr. Richard Hooker: With an Account of His Life and Death by Isaac Walton*. 3 vols. Oxford: Oxford University Press, 1836.

Kindred-Barnes, Scott. *Richard Hooker's Use of History in His Defense of Public Worship: His Anglican Critique of Calvin, Barrow, and the Puritans*. Lewiston: Mellen, 2011.

Kindred-Barnes, Scott, and W. Bradford Littlejohn, eds. *Richard Hooker and Reformed Orthodoxy*. Reformed Historical Theology series. Göttingen: Vandenhoeck & Ruprecht, forthcoming 2016.

Kirby, W. J., ed. *A Companion to Richard Hooker*. Leiden: Brill, 2008.

———. "From 'Generall Meditations' to 'Particular Decisions': The Augustinian Coherence of Richard Hooker's Political Theology." In *Law and Sovereignty in the Middle Ages and the Renaissance*, edited by Robert S. Sturges, 41–63. Arizona Studies in the Middle Ages and the Renaissance 28. Turnhout: Brepols, 2011.

———, ed. *Richard Hooker and the English Reformation*. Dordrecht: Kluwer Academic, 2003.

———. *Richard Hooker, Reformer and Platonist*. Aldershot: Ashgate, 2005.

———. *Richard Hooker's Doctrine of the Royal Supremacy*. Leiden: Brill, 1990.

———. "The 'sundrie waies of Wisdom': Richard Hooker on the Authority of Scripture and Reason." In *Oxford Handbook of the Bible in Early Modern England, c.* 1530–1700, Kevin Killeen et al., eds. Oxford: Oxford University Press, forthcoming 2015.

Lake, Peter. *Anglicans and Puritans? Presbyterianism and English Conformist Thought from Whitgift to Hooker.* London: Unwin Hyman, 1988.

———. "Business as Usual? The Immediate Reception of Hooker's Ecclesiastical Polity." *Journal of Ecclesiastical History* 52.3 (2001) 456–86.

———. *Moderate Puritans and the Elizabethan Church.* Cambridge: Cambridge University Press, 1982.

———. "Puritanism, Arminianism, and Nicholas Tyacke." Introduction to *Religious Politics in Post-Reformation England: Essays in Honour of Nicholas Tyacke*, edited by Kenneth Fincham and Peter Lake, 1–15. Woodbridge, Suffolk: Boydell, 2006.

Lewis, C. S. *English Literature in the Sixteenth Century, Excluding Drama.* Oxford History of English Literature 3. Oxford: Clarendon, 1954.

Littlejohn, W. Bradford. "Bancroft *versus* Penry: Conscience and Authority in Elizabethan Polemics." In W. J. Torrance Kirby and P. G. Stanwood, eds., *Paul's Cross and the Culture of Persuasion in England,* 1520–1640, 327–44. Leiden: Brill, 2014.

———. *The Freedom of a Christian Commonwealth: Richard Hooker and the Problem of Christian Liberty.* Emory University Studies in Law and Religion. Grand Rapids: Eerdmans, forthcoming 2016.

———. "More than a Swineherd: Hooker, Vermigli, and the Aristotelian Defense of the Royal Supremacy." *Reformation and Renaissance Review* 15.1 (2014) 78–93.

———. "Richard Hooker, Franciscus Junius, and a Reformed Theology of Law." In Kindred-Barnes and Littlejohn, eds., *Richard Hooker and Reformed Orthodoxy.*

———. "The Search for a Reformed Hooker: Some Modest Proposals." *Reformation and Renaissance Review* 16.1 (2015) 68–82.

———. "The Use and Abuse of John Jewel in Richard Hooker's Defense of the English Church." In *Defending the Faith: John Jewel and the Church of England,* edited by Angela Ranson and Andre Gazal. Kirksville, MO: Truman State University Press, forthcoming 2015.

Bibliography

Lowrie, Walter. *The Church and Its Organization in Primitive and Catholic Times: An Interpretation of Rudolph Sohm's Kirchenrecht.* Vol. 1. New York: Longmans, 1904.

Luther, Martin. *On the Freedom of a Christian* (1520). Edited by Harold J. Grimm. In *Luther's Works: American Edition*, vol. 31, *Career of the Reformer I*. St. Louis: Concordia; Philadelphia: Muhlenberg, 1955–.

———. *Treatise on Good Works* (1520). Translated by W. A. Lambert. Edited by James Atkinson. In *Luther's Works: American Edition*, vol. 44, *The Christian in Society I*. St. Louis: Concordia; Philadelphia: Muhlenberg, 1955–.

Lynch, Michael J. "Richard Hooker and the Development of English Hypothetical Universalism." In Kindred-Barnes and Littlejohn, eds., *Richard Hooker and Reformed Orthodoxy*.

MacCulloch, Diarmaid. *The Later Reformation in England, 1547–1603.* Basingstoke: Palgrave MacMillan, 2001.

———. *Reformation: Europe's House Divided, 1490–1700.* London: Allen Lane, 2003.

———. "Richard Hooker's Reputation." In Kirby, ed., *A Companion to Richard Hooker*, 563–610.

McCullough, Peter, ed. *Lancelot Andrewes: Selected Sermons and Lectures.* Oxford: Oxford University Press, 2005.

McGrade, A. S. "Classical, Patristic, and Medieval Sources." In Kirby, ed., *A Companion to Richard Hooker*, 51–88.

———, ed. *Of the Laws of Ecclesiastical Polity.* Critical edition with modern spelling. 3 vols. Oxford: Oxford University Press, 2013.

———, ed. *Richard Hooker and the Construction of Christian Community.* Tempe, AZ: Medieval & Renaissance Texts & Studies, 1997.

Miller, Charles. *Richard Hooker and the Vision of God: Exploring the Origins of "Anglicanism."* Cambridge: Clarke, 2013.

Milton, Anthony. *The British Delegation and the Synod of Dort (1618–1619).* Woodbridge: Boydell, 2005.

Morris, Christopher. Introduction to *Of the Laws of Ecclesiastical Polity.* 2 vols. London: Dent, 1907.

Muller, Richard A. *After Calvin: Studies in the Development of a Theological Tradition.* Oxford: Oxford University Press, 2003.

———. Review of *English Hypothetical Universalism: John Preston and the Softening of Reformed Theology*, by Jonathan D. Moore. *Calvin Theological Journal* 43.1 (2008) 149–50.

———. *The Unaccommodated Calvin: Studies in the Foundation of a Theological Tradition.* Oxford: Oxford University Press, 2000.

Neelands, W. David. "Christology and the Sacraments." In Kirby, ed., *A Companion to Richard Hooker*, 369–402.

———. "Hooker on Scripture, Reason, and 'Tradition.'" In McGrade, ed., *Richard Hooker and the Construction of Christian Community*, 75–94.

———. "Predestination." In Kirby, ed., *A Companion to Richard Hooker*, 185–220.

———. "Richard Hooker on the Identity of the Visible and Invisible Church." In Kirby, ed., *Richard Hooker and the English Reformation*, 99–110.

———. "Richard Hooker's Paul's Cross Sermon." In Kirby and Stanwood, eds., *Paul's Cross and the Culture of Persuasion*, 245–62.

O'Donovan, Joan Lockwood. *Theology of Law and Authority in the English Reformation*. Emory University Studies in Law and Religion 1. Atlanta: Scholars, 1991.

O'Donovan, Oliver. "What Kind of Community Is the Church? The Richard Hooker Lectures 2005." *Ecclesiology* 3.2 (2007) 171–93.

Pearson, A. F. Scott. *Church & State: Political Aspects of Sixteenth Century Puritanism*. Cambridge: Cambridge University Press, 1928.

———. *Thomas Cartwright and Elizabethan Puritanism, 1535–1603*. Gloucester, MA: Smith, 1966.

Porter, Jean. *Nature as Reason: A Thomistic Theory of the Natural Law*. Grand Rapids: Eerdmans, 2005.

Shagan, Ethan. *Rule of Moderation: Violence, Religion, and the Politics of Restraint in Early Modern England*. Cambridge: Cambridge University Press, 2011.

Shuger, Debora K. "Faith and Assurance." In Kirby, ed., *A Companion to Richard Hooker*, 221–50.

Skinner, Quentin. *Foundations of Modern Political Thought*. Vol. 2, *The Age of Reformation*. Cambridge: Cambridge University Press, 1978.

Snoddy, Richard. *The Soteriology of James Ussher: The Act and Object of Saving Faith*. Oxford: Oxford University Press, 2014.

Thompson, W. D. J. Cargill. "The Philosopher of the 'Politic Society': Richard Hooker as Political Thinker." In Hill, ed., *Studies in Richard Hooker*, 3–76.

Travers, Walter. *A Full and Plaine Declaration of Ecclesiasticall Discipline Owt Off the Word Off God / and Off the Declininge Off the Churche Off England From the Same*. Zurich: Froschauer, 1574.

Bibliography

Verkamp, Bernard J. *The Indifferent Mean: Adiaphorism in the English Reformation to 1554.* Athens: Ohio University Press, 1977.

Voak, Nigel. *Richard Hooker and Reformed Theology: A Study of Reason, Will, and Grace.* Oxford: Oxford University Press, 2003.

Voegelin, Eric. *The New Science of Politics: An Introduction.* Walgreen Foundation Lectures. Foreword by Dante Germino. Chicago: University of Chicago Press, 1987.

Whitgift, John. *Whitgift's Works.* Edited by John Ayre. 3 vols. Cambridge: Parker Society, 1849–51.

Witte, John E., Jr. *Law and Protestantism: The Legal Teachings of the Lutheran Reformation.* Cambridge; New York: Cambridge University Press, 2002.

Wright, N. T. *The Last Word: Beyond the Bible Wars to a New Understanding of the Authority of Scripture.* Grand Rapids: Zondervan, 2005.

Zanchi, Girolamo. "On the Law in General." Translated by Jeffrey J. Veenstra. *Journal of Markets and Morality* 6.1 (2003) 305–98.